Beyond Shopper
Marketing

Colin F. Harper B.Sc. M.A.

To Frankie and the team without whom none of this would be possible, and to Carolyne Wahlen, who provided the inspiration.

About the Author

Colin Harper was educated at Bishop Veseys Grammar School in Sutton Coldfield, and gained a B.Sc in Psychology from Manchester University, followed by an M.A. in Marketing from Lancaster University.

Having spent 10 years with brand marketing - the BAT subsidiary, British American Cosmetics and Guinness Group, he then changed from the brand side to work with a variety of Sales Promotion Agencies rising to MD.

In 1995 he set up Storecheck Marketing Ltd. Having noticed the huge gap between retailer promises of action and delivered results, this company was launched alongside a major piece of research showing that actual compliance to POP and agreed store placement of added off shelf space was as low as 50%.

These figures are now widely accepted as a regrettable fact. Storecheck – set up with the objective of "giving companies everything they need to get growth in store", has continued to be at the leading edge of point of purchase research. Storecheck research has been used widely including by industry bodies such as The Grocer and the IGD.

Colin served on the POPAI (Point of Purchase Advertising International) research committee, working with major brands to deliver cutting edge insight into best practise at the point of purchase.

Colin was then invited to become part time Head of Insight for the IPM (Institute of Promotional Marketing) – a post he held for 3 years. In that role, he produced 4 White Papers, including one, "In Place of Price" that outlined the long term benefits of alternatives to simple price discounting.

He works with the University of Kent Value Chain MSc course, as well as with their Ph.D. students.

He is actively involved in developing big data insights into the point of purchase as the key means of developing brand growth, leading to the recent launch of RetailVitalStatistics.com.

Contents

Forward

It was Edwina Dunn, co-founder of dunnhumby (of Tesco Clubcard fame), who once said, "The more targeted the offer, the fewer gimmicks you need to sell it. It will sell itself because it is what people want." And it was Jacqui Hill, Unilever's Marketing Development Director, who said, "Between us, marketers and retailers have trained an entire generation of shoppers to only buy on promotion. It's not that they need to, but why shouldn't they when price deals are available on key brands so often? Future generations may well look back on this as a time of anti-marketing unless we take action now."

Price promotions are dangerous to the FMCG industry. They contribute to waste and obesity, and they diminish profitability along the retail food chain. Unless something is done soon, the government will have no choice but to regulate the retail industry. Some fear the government may go as far as to banish the BOGOF entirely, and put the brakes on the "race to the bottom" the retail industry appears hell-bent on pursuing. Nobody wants to see that happen, and many question the desire within government to take on such a powerful sector. In order to prevent this from coming to pass, the retail industry needs to marshal all the evidence in favour of a sustainable competitive advantage. If marketers and account managers do not break their addiction to short-term volume uplifts and capacity utilisation, the negative effect on the retail industry could be permanent.

It is ironic that an industry obsessed with lean thinking should be so blind to the implications of relying upon promotions as a business strategy. A lean-focused organisation thrives when the end consumer has predictable demands the industry can meet. The retail industry, as it currently stands, does the opposite. It fuels demand amplification, and creates uncertainty within the market. The best way to ensure the health of the retail sector is to encourage stable and predictable demand, and to reduce volatility and unplanned variation in price as much as possible. Agility in manufacturing, distribution and retailing comes at a cost, and this is a reality that the FMCG industry appears reluctant (or unable) to accept.

I hope this book will serve as a timely reminder of the alternatives to price promotions, and the barriers manufacturers and retailers must overcome in order to continue to make promotions a viable long-term business strategy. Colin Harper is a visionary and a pragmatist – he sees that which is invisible to most. This book provides invaluable insight into the theory behind damaging marketing trends, and an escape route from the cycle of constant price promotions.

Professor Andrew Fearne

Centre for Value Chain Research
Kent Business School, University of Kent

Chapter 1

Why Do You Need this Book?

There are many books on marketing strategy. This is not one of them.

It is about how you can deliver results NOW and on into the future at the same time. A strategic approach to the tactical necessities faced by every company, every year.

This is about consistently and continuously delivering targets

Price discounting is the most prevalent form of promotional incentive in the UK. While it is demonised by many parties, and expensive to use it is not going to go away in a hurry. It is also, as we will see, inextricably built into the brand plans of many companies.

For the smart company, alternatives exist. They deliver better value for money (VFM), can also be built around discounting, and take account of the importance of retail groups to brand planning.

Retailers are actually central to a brand strategy. In their own way they are as important as consumers, and the approach that we suggest brings the two together. This book is just the leading edge of a drive to bring retailers and brands together to satisfy customers, and also to generate a foundation for mutual growth. This plan can be signed up to at all levels in the company, because it is inclusive, measured, and can be shown to work.

Working with the Retail Bulletin – the leading retail news website, there is a new sub-site appearing: "In Place of Price"
www.theretailbulletin.com/inplaceofprice

Turn here whenever you want to get more information on growth away from simple, but expensive, discounting.

It's about spending money smarter

August bodies like the IPA (The Institute of Practitioners in Advertising) see that work currently considered to be tactical - such as promotions – can be a very important element of delivering against a strategic goal. In a seminar, one of their report authors commented that "advertising and promotions are a marriage made in heaven".

If you are an award winner in their annual contest, either by design or by accident, you got it right. You can see by the absence of year on year winners though, that if winning was by design, it was not a design that stood the test of time.

Cynically, but probably accurately, you could say that no-one wants the same companies cropping up year on year. Just glancing round the industry it is hard to see companies that stand out as getting it right all the time.

Few companies have so much money that they can simply fling it around and hope some of it sticks. Most companies have a finite budget chasing too many objectives.

If you fall into the former category, please don't bother reading this book; just spend anywhere that takes your fancy and then take a long holiday. This will leave a little bit of space for the rest of us to eke out our budgets.

Given that by now we have lost people to whom value for money, and guaranteed delivery against targets is a completely abstract concept, let's get down to basics.

I spent three years as Head of Insight for the Institute of Promotional Marketing, following hard on the heels of being on the POPAI research committee, viewing and researching the impact of promotions and point of purchase material day in, day out for some years.

On top of this, my own company, Storecheck Marketing Ltd. carries out and evaluates promotion activity as a core function.

Through wearing all of these hats I get the results of nitty gritty activity running past me all the time. I have rendered this down into a set of recommendations based simply on two things. The likelihood of success, and the attendant ROI. There are activities that can be very successful. Off-shelf cardboard displays are one. But a national campaign based on these with, as an example, leaflets, has such a low probability of successful placement that it may not be worth considering. On the other hand, there are activities that will deliver, but are so expensive that the low return on investment (ROI) takes them out of contention.

The other area I am familiar with is the overall lack of promotional measurement. I have heard through agencies requests from brands for supporting information for one approach or another. Almost always these are coupled with the fact that the brands have not measured any of their back activity, and have no plans to do so in the future.

Almost everyone using promotions wants to find someone out there who has measured, and is prepared to share.

In the POP area, I have sat in rooms with retailers, brands, agencies, and POP manufacturers. Without exception, they all turn to each other for insight, but neither retailers nor brands professed themselves willing to share the sales data that would make such measurement possible.

So right round the industry there is total and complete agreement on one thing. Everyone wants information on what works, and no-one is prepared to provide any!

Having said that, information does exist in pockets. Certainly my company, Storecheck, has developed a great deal; the IPM have some, as do POPAI. In fact POPAI has carried out some really groundbreaking cross industry work on what POP works and where.

I am indebted to all of these people, and more who will be credited as their contribution is used, for the facts you will find in the following pages.

My company has also launched a new website: ***RetailVitalStatistics.com***, designed to promote "fishing where the fish are".

Across the years it has become obvious that retailers are torn between wanting to direct everything that happens in the store, and the realisation that it is not only an impossible dream, but also an unnatural one.

People live in ghettoes. These can be upmarket, like Knightsbridge, or downmarket, like Hackney. The very first piece of vital information is about your core customers, and the core stores that serve them. Different of course, for every brand.

The same size of store, but completely different traffic and needs typify the stores, and the areas they serve. The degree of flexibility in ranging that a local independent store used to be able to offer is unmanageable against a central model. The current stock control systems were born in the heady days of the turn of the century, when multiples gnawed away at independent sales. In the modern era of multi-format stores they have become a dinosaur.

Actually, dinosaurs are a closer analogy than it would at first appear. Like the retailer supply chain, there was a vast distance between the head office and the tail. Some dinosaurs seem to have managed that distance by having a subsidiary brain nearer that point of action.

Some retailers are re-discovering the value of empowering the store. Oh, of course, you will have bad managers, and of course you will have mistakes made. But there is nothing like a system to really make a mess (SNAFU).

It's all about Price Discounting isn't it?

Well, actually, it is, but no-one seems to be happy about it. It is, in fact, just an expensive variant of a free gift with purchase, but price discounting has become the most prevalent promotion incentive in the UK.

Retailers say they don't like it, but their customers demand it. Manufacturers insist either that their competitors or the retailers are actually responsible. Informed observers like KPMG have been saying for some time that the level of discounting is unsustainable. Clearly this is not the case, since the levels of discounts continue to rise.

Notwithstanding this position, many brands go public with their dislike. Recently P&G boss Irwin Lee was quoted in The Grocer as saying that he was "kept awake at night" by the amount of promotional offers, which he said was "ever deepening". He reported that over 80% of volume was sold on deals, compared to 66% five years ago. "We believe", he added, that "promotions win quarters, but true innovation wins decades".

As a counterweight to this, a letter writer called John Eustace, commenting on the article, remembered back to 1972. He recalled that Jim Tappen, then MD, announced that they were pulling out of promotions altogether. The writer then said that this lasted for just one Nielsen period, by which point the P&G share had dropped to just 34%. Result: an immediate reversal.

N.B. "Those who cannot remember the past are condemned to repeat it". (George Santayana)

What appears to be happening is that retailers and brands are innovating to decrease the value for money (VFM) of their unpromoted product.

This can be done either by increasing the price, so that half-price is at a realistic level, or by decreasing the product weight, thereby making the discounted level affordable. The former happens in areas where size change is an issue, such as wines and spirits, the latter in more flexible production areas such as crisps.

The net result, of course, is that brands taking this approach have a certain level of discounting and volume that they must reach. In this position their margin is much more finely balanced, and a full price strategy is out of reach.

Discounting is integral, and cannot easily be wound back.

Finding the Win Win Win

Accepting that promotions are inevitable, the requirement is to bring targeting and organisation into the way they are run, and the selection of approaches that build, not destroy.

The Win Win Win position comes when, as you spend a pound (or a dollar), it impacts at every point that can influence the buying or selling decision for your product.

The consumer, the shopper and the store

Beyond Shopper Marketing

Shopper Marketing concerns itself with the shopper, and anything that has a bearing on their relationship with the product. Beyond Shopper Marketing recognises the very real importance of this, but also understands the crippled nature of the store systems serving 21st century supply chains.

Beyond Shopper Marketing recognises the sheer impossibility of changing everything, everywhere, and shows you ways of changing everything – consumer, shopper and store conditions, where it will make the most difference to you.

You move the shoppers, and you advise the store that you are spending to build sales in their store, so they had better shape up to take advantage. You take the results for the stores back centrally and introduce change nationally.

There are many other ways to deliver this effect (shoppers and stores local synergy) with a message that will play really well centrally. We call this effect, ZYNERGY, bringing in the third, Z axis of a chart – store and supply chain spend – alongside the effect of consumer advertising and store based media.

One activity, amplified 3 times

Zynergy is as much about measurement as it is action. Measurement convinces others, and the one thing you will need is to have a firm basis you can share to make partners out of colleagues, and supporters out of customers.

This book is all about enhancing, and delivering this zynergy. Where every pound you spend delivers for you on every level, and every action is evaluated against its likely effect all round.

Stick to the Facts

Double jeopardy is an empirical law in marketing where, with few exceptions, the lower market share brands in a market have both far fewer buyers in a time period, and also lower brand loyalty. Ehrenburg, who coined the law, based it on a vast number of statistically significant readings over many years.

It suggests that, if you want to grow, don't focus on trying to hang on to the customers you have: look outside for new ones. The more customers you have, the more will exhibit loyalty in the way they buy.

The Ehrenburg-Bass Institute, supported by many of the leading FMCG companies internationally, continues his research. Byron Sharp from the Institute, writing in "How Brands Grow", identifies achieving high actual and virtual availability as the key marketing task - making a brand easy to buy.

His comment is that anything else is secondary.

The following chapters stick to facts, and focus on building a brand using the simple principles espoused by Ehrenberg and Byron Sharp.

Build more users, and be more visible in more places.

Post Script

In the pages that follow I touch on a number of issues where you may feel you would like to learn more. If so, you can buy my new textbook on this issue, written in conjunction with Roddy Mullin. Shoppernomics (Gower Publications) adds very significantly to the approach outlined in this book.

You can also e-mail me for access to a Dropbox of some of the resources referred to in the book: ***results@storecheck.co.uk***

Chapter 2

We're busy going nowhere, isn't it just a crime?*

A city dweller, who we will call Richard, was making his first trip to the country. So naturally he went prepared. Plenty of food and drink, a full tank of petrol, and, most important of all, a fully charged satnav. Of course, he had heard the horror stories. The destination 10 miles down the road routed via a ferry to Cork. And the 10 wheeler sent down a single track cul-de-sac for 10 miles. But then, it never happens to you.

Except, this time, it did. After some time fruitlessly navigating the back roads of an idyllic maze overgrown with trees, and no sign of a GPS signal, or a way out, Richard was relieved to find a local leaning on a gate.

Parking the car carefully avoiding the overgrown ditches at the side of the road, he picked his way carefully over the rutted verge, and made his way to the gate.

"Am I pleased to see you, I'm completely lost and trying to find my way to" -- and here he mentioned the name of a village that could not be more than a few miles away.

The local – wearing a well-used pair of wellies and a somewhat blank expression, turned his head to look Richard straight in the eye.

* *A line from a song entitled – "Busy doing nothing working the whole day through...".*

"Well sorr", he opined, "if you wanted to get there you wouldn't want to start from here".

It has often surprised me how many excellent companies are quite happy to set off into a new financial year with no knowledge of where they are, but with a precise knowledge of where they would like to go.

Here I have to confess to having been party to the same mistake myself. Having been in the sales promotion business for some time, I had grown used to tactical activity.

For those not aware of tactical promotions, they are basically subsets of a year plan entered into with a separate objective of some description. This objective may, or may not, be realisable. What it typically is not, is measured.

In fact, as it was entered into at a relatively low level in the organisation, this did not really seem to matter.

Often the rate of staff promotion or re-location meant that someone different was in place at the end than at the beginning. There are often complaints by agencies that the process by which tactical promotions were accepted means that an agency with a great - indeed IPM award winning promotion – would not get the nod for the next. In fact, when I followed through on one year's winners, only 50% of the agencies were in place the following year.

You take on board in promotions the relative impermanence of relationships, and you accept a constant series of last minute changes of plan, or new business quotes based on entirely new briefs, since the old approach has, for whatever reason, been discarded. Meanwhile the heady search is for the new and the untried, since the only permanence is change.

The main thrust of this book is to lay out a cost effective research base giving companies a real framework to grow from. This is based on the best regarded industry practise, and also gives measures for actually evaluating your performance.

I then go on to lay out a basis for growth which has, coincidentally just been announced by Coca Cola. It is designed to focus on core areas of brand support.

The press release said: "The customer insight initiative will see the business create a network of outlets over the next three years that either currently sell or have the potential to sell its brands. The platform garners sales and volume data which Coke will combine with its own before mapping it against external consumer, workplace, competitor and retail geo-demographics".

In effect, Coca-Cola is making each shop a major customer ... and treating them appropriately.

This is the same Coke which recently launched a 250 ml can at 49p as opposed to 65p for the 330 ml as a reaction to 25p a can when bought as an eight-pack in supermarkets. Someone is listening and learning.

Irwin Lee, the P&G boss referred to in the last chapter discussed using the "power of our innovations, the power of the multichannel environment, and the power of business intelligence technologies to drive a more sustainable growth agenda".

Coca Cola obviously believe that what is needed is innovation in marketing to build core growth on top of innovation in product, addressing price promotion issues.

Chapter 3

Sustainable Growth from Your Core

A number of companies have grown very successfully by consolidating one area and becoming strong, then moving on. Walkers and Warburtons spring immediately to mind. Distribution, distance and freshness were probably deciding factors in the way that they grew, but their key competitors – Golden Wonder and British and Allied Bakeries – could not easily counter their growth, as they had the whole country to worry about.

Today, the "area" that you use and treat as a core could be as low as a single person. The rapid growth of alternative direct media, and of the means to immediately measure the impact of what you do, gives much greater flexibility. Social media allows people to talk about small successes, and to cover the country overnight.

You will see, though, that it is retailers and shoppers together that give you the growth that you need. As a result your realistic minimum core area is that defined by the catchment area of your core stores.

Your core areas, based on epos data, can become increasingly larger proportions of your total sales. This will be based on increases in your original stores and the added sales brought in by new stores in the same area.

To put this in perspective, for any one product, three small stores are typically equal to one large one. With this in mind it should be relatively easy to double the sales in a typical core area.

In terms of spend, it is much easier to look like a brand leader in a smaller area than ever before. £100,000 across the United Kingdom is a drop in the ocean. Spread around 10 core areas, possibly 80-100 stores, a few hundred thousand households, perhaps 30% of your business, where you know exactly where people live, it's simple.

Factor into that a build of distribution, plus the knowledge you will gain of what worked, and you have a basis that will allow you to grow with confidence.

All of this is dependent on having some basic data to work from. This needs to inform:

- the company, and
- the three main drivers for growth
  - the shopper
  - the local store
  - the retail buyers and supply chain

For the shopper, you have marketing messaging and the whole range of tools available to you. In the kind of targeted marketing we discuss, the impact is easy to see.

For the store, you need more stores and additional space, improving real and virtual availability (you need to be seen everywhere).

For the retailer buyers, you bring them the good news that you will be growing – and how. You can also bring them some unique insights they can get nowhere else.

There are many misconceptions about what can be achieved in all the areas above; these are addressed in the following pages.

I have sat in meetings where senior marketing personnel deny the existence of store by store epos data (in one case a director was immediately corrected by the sales director sitting opposite). I have known of very large companies, where access to this data is jealously guarded. I have been in meetings with sales personnel who claimed to have no idea that epos data existed, or denied their ability to engage with supply chain in any way. Many more do not see availability as an issue for them, or indeed important in any way. Others do not understand what the data is actually saying to them, or feel they do not have time to understand it.

There follow some really simple ways to use data you already have. If you are time poor, insight can be bought in. Many companies profess they are allergic to investment in insight – "after all we could", they say, "put all of this into discounting". It is precisely a lack of proper measurement that leaves companies in the position they are in at the moment. If the sales department cannot find the budget to measure the benefit of investment, eventually, the shareholders will. Better perhaps, that finance or the MD ring fence a way forward.

There are also other simple, and, in the grand scheme of things, inexpensive, measures that have the dual function of directing your investment while being of great use to your retailer partner. You will need them on side at all levels if you are to realise best ROI.

Because of the comprehensive lack of measurement in the area, companies seeking a way back from the ever more rapid growth of discounting have not developed an armoury of alternative techniques that work. No matter what companies want, there will be no immediate roll back to the 1990's. Actually, all you need to be is better than your competitors. Other promotion techniques are much more cost efficient than discounting, and if you improve your discount performance you will get more, for less.

Fact based growth, though, will often be impossible unless companies actually question their current assumptions.

Chapter 4

"Elementary, My Dear Watson"

Sherlock Holmes never said this, and he was certainly not the first to be misquoted. Much of what we firmly believe is drawn from "facts" we have been sold. This is possibly because they came from a seemingly credible source, but with a hidden agenda, such as: "eat up, crusts make your hair curl".

In the words of the former United States Secretary of Defense, Donald Rumsfeld, "There are known knowns; there are things we know that we know. There are known unknowns; that is to say, there are things that we now know we don't know. But there are also unknown unknowns – there are things we do not know we don't know."

He should have added to this, "and there are also false knowns"; that is to say, things that we believe to be the truth that are actually untrue. On his watch, the Iraq war actually cost the US Government $843,542,436,929 according to the Iraq War Clock – a figure that increases every second as the repercussions echo on.

This war was entered into for many reasons, but the one most cited by the governments taking part was the belief that Iraq possessed Weapons of Mass Destruction (WMD), ready to be used at any moment. The research into this, carried out by putting troops and tanks on the ground, was an extremely expensive way of exposing this "known" as false. If what you really need is market research, then there are other ways of finding out; committing heavy expenditure into terra incognito is not one.

This is the **"Rumsfeld Effect": An expensive mistaken action based on unquestioned belief.**

We don't want to do this.

The question is, what should you know about the store?

For many companies the store is a little bit like the old maps of the world: some known areas imprecisely laid out and vast swathes of territory where there would be pictures of sea monsters. We may not ever know everything about the world, but we can understand the things that matter.

How well does the store actually support my sales?

Well, the store is a market in more ways than one. Yes, they are a super-market for their customers; they lay out their goods in part to a pre-arranged plan developed often hundreds of miles away.

In practise, for many stores, this varies wildly from a central plan if they end up serving e-commerce. On-line sales are becoming an increasingly important feature of the retail environment. For some stores 15% or more of their sales could serve customers who never set foot there from one week to another.

E-commerce orders also act as market research. It is very noticeable that, in flagrant disregard of the whole of the rest of the web, the major grocery retailers do not seek feedback from their customers. Their customers, though, denied that courtesy, complain to each other. Nowadays, customers with attitude can vent this on a multitude of web sites, and there are now companies, (I use SpectrumInsight), who can tell you exactly what they are saying.

The advantages of trawling the web for feedback are many. There is no hint of bias, since they are not answering a potentially loaded question. What SpectrumInsight do is to get every mention of a retail group, and then look at the context against data dictionaries which they compile.

Using this approach, they are able to say with 100% confidence that if you take out reported issues with deliveries, and the website, the next largest issue for all the major retailers in the UK is substitutions. Here is a sample of their feedback (spelling and layout as entered):

- I think the Tesco work-experience kid packed my online grocery order. fish Pie Mix substituted for mussels in coriander, chilli and lime

- What makes you think you can substitute turkey for frozen fish cakes in my delivery? Why? Simply awful #asda #groceries

- Thanks Sainsburys. I ordered Spot On for cats, you substituted Spot On for puppies with a huge red label saying DO NOT USE ON CATS

- my first supermarket delivery – was quite excited, but @sainsburys was late and had substituted half the items, so it'll cost more. Hmm

- Tesco delivery changed man. They're all about lateness, crappy substitutions and arsey delivery drivers now. Sainsburys next time it is

Accept, please, that in some stores the fact that you are core, perhaps combined with e-commerce, will mean that you lose sales, probably very significantly.

SpectrumInsight has developed for us a summary view of customers actually complaining about product availability. They refer to retail outlets across the course of the year. This is available from the Dropbox resource mentioned at the beginning of this book. Clearly, this varies across the course of the year in line with demand. There are, though, distinct differences between retailers. Asda have particular issues with home entertainment, but they all had problems at Easter 2013 with Easter Eggs. A Telegraph report suggested that readers should buy at Christmas instead.

Also accept that the last quote, suggesting a planned change from Tesco to Sainsbury, is something that stores should not want to hear. But it is also something that you should not want to hear either. When a shopper switches store they lose a customer. Similarly you do not also lose only one sale if yours is the substituted product. The one sale you are not making is multiplied by the fact that you are not available in the store, which means you also lose there. Plus, the people who you know wanted to buy yours are now forced to trial competitive products.

If you take the view that you can do nothing about this, please stop reading now. If you take this view because that is what your company tells you, I would look around for another job. If you are measured by results, you are not going to be able to do much with your hands tied.

The store is a market in its own right.

Clearly you need to research what they believe, and what the store management can and cannot achieve.

Basic Store Research

This splits neatly into two areas: (1) what a manager can do on his own, and (2) what store systems impose on the position.

What can a manager do on his own

A store manager is torn between implementing systems, satisfying customers and delivering his profit targets. If you talk to them, you will also discover that they feel bedevilled by meetings. Meetings from people calling on the store, and internal meetings. All of these get in the way of being able to implement systems and shopper requests.

Store managers complain that they have too little resource to implement everything, and that a day manager has absolutely no control over what the night shift does.

Any good manager will respond to change if it is presented as if it matters to him. Importantly, the extent of change that they can make is extensive, IF and only IF they actually believe it will benefit their store over and above their closest competitors, local managers coming under the same regional manager.

The easy way to find out what store managers can impact in your area is to ask them. But don't just ask one. Ask a number, and when you do, focus on stores where you could really make a difference – check out Chapter 5 (the definition of a core store) before you start here. For all new clients Storecheck ask a number of questions that uncover where investment can impact on your sales directly. They do this by telephone, since you can ring back when a manager is able to take the call. It may be up to three times but managers are always grateful when you think about them. Do not just expect them to drop everything. You would not expect this from a customer, and in their role, they are your customer.

This is a selection from the standard questionnaire (scores are those agreeing):

Do you recognise that your store is a core Store? 55%
  – Many alert managers recognise they have issues well before you do.

Would you find it useful to receive information in the post? 93%
  – Note that only named mail is likely to get through.

Would your store be interested in hosting in-store tastings? 86%
  – You may feel that only official expensive tastings are available. This is untrue – collaborative tastings are available in other areas of the store.

Would you find it useful if we were to send you free samples for you and your colleagues to try (in store or at home with family members)? 94%
  – Not only are staff potential customers, they also refill your shelves.

Would you find it useful to be advised in advance when coupon drops are happening around your store? 92%
- Store managers know that these really work, and they get really annoyed when customers turn up, can't buy and blame them for something they know nothing about.

Are you an on-line store? 53%
- It won't surprise you that for many brands the double stress of normal AND e-commerce sales will beat systems. However, this stress also represents a real opportunity to grow.

Would you find it useful if a merchandiser were to leave behind a bespoke promotion after the call? 56%
- Check Chapter 11.

Would you find a bespoke shipper useful to maximise space in store? 39%
- Yes, they can take their own.

Would you be able to increase your shelf cap to pull more stock into your store? 81%
- There are always a few that actually don't know how to do this. They can be helped.

How useful have you found this call on a scale of 1 to 10 (10 being very useful)? Average 8
- Storecheck always ask how useful a store has found a contact. In the event that this figure is less than 6 they stop immediately. I am always surprised that this question is not included in every store contact. More than anything else it lets you know if you are going to get action as a result, and the value of your investment in the activity.

You may immediately think – "Aaah, must pick up the phone and talk to a field marketing company". This would be another example of the

"Rumsfeld Effect". Standard Field Marketing per se will achieve no more for you now than it has in the past. What you need is a comprehensive and continuous store contact strategy. Field marketing may well have a place here, but only in answer to some very specific issues, and delivering more than one store benefit.

Your budget needs to deliver much more.

ACTION: Research your core stores. See the Core Stores section to understand how to find these.

What do systems impose on stores that you need to know, and can affect?

Every stock control system varies. I give you a few facts that are true as I write, but might not be true when you read. It is very much up to you to find out.

In Tescolink, their computer screen that says "listed stores not selling" does not mean that, rather unfortunately, the store did not sell this week. It actually means that the store has never set the product up on their stock computer, and it will never sell. Similarly, the screen that says "listed stores selling" does not mean they sold. It simply means that the store computer has been set it up so that the store can order. Simply wander down this screen to assure yourself that there are typically a few zeroes. If those zeros last for more than about six weeks, the store computer will simply archive the product. It will never sell in that store again. BUT it will still be listed as selling.

There are many reasons a product will stop selling. This could include a competitor taking your Shelf Edge Label (SEL) off the shelf!

In Asda, they have a DD rate of sale. This is supposed to register the lowest rate of sale for a non-promoted product. They have so many promotions that often this level is based on a promoted period. This means they don't increase allocations when a promotion does come along. The consequence: instant underperformance.

In Sainsbury, the only way you can track by store performance is through the Big Button. It is only available for the current week, so immediate store insight is limited. It should arrive on the Tuesday but often misses days, and might be as much as a week late. They don't tell you the stores that should be stocking. One way to identify this is to check the stores that have stock as you get a listing, and then look at their performance over time. Some brands find they are told they can't get this. Inadequate though it is, it is the best available and persistence usually pays off.

In Morrisons, the data is much less available, and also much less useful, as it includes only one sales measure, and no stock.

Other available data is from the Co-op and Boots, both at a cost.

ALL the store groups have issues with stores stopping selling, although typically, Asda systems are best at managing this issue, as managers get a special report on this issue.

ACTION: Get all the data you can, understand what it means, and plan to manage immediately the issues that it raises.

What happens at the facing of your stores?

Where you are stocked on the shelf makes a big difference to how you sell. The POP that your retailer places makes a big difference to whether or not shoppers actually take time out to look at your shelf (look at Chapter 8: "POP and other In-Store media" for information about this).

If you want to do better, the first place you look is the facing. So if you have a store group underperforming, start there by seeing how shoppers find the category.

Interestingly, shelves are re-laid in consultation, typically with category captains. After a relay, everyone breathes a sigh of relief and starts on the next one. It is not usual to see and analyse how they actually perform in practice. The results of looking at a facing properly can be very profitable. Storecheck managed a relay for the adult soft drinks area (J20, Shloer etc.) in Asda. There was a 30% increase in sales between before and after. This was linked to re-blocking, and the simple addition of bus stops to make navigation easier. (Too few people actually looked at the area, and simply improving visibility improved sales!)

How do you understand your shoppers and the section?

Realistically, the only way to do this is to video the shopper in action. Not only can this be analysed and digitised later BUT nothing convinces like video clips.

To achieve this you actually need to be able to match up your own category against all others. What percentage of the store traffic actually shop the aisle? Of these, how many look? How many approach? And of these, how many buy?

The POPAI work in Chapter 8 was based on people with video headsets tracking round a store. But better for a single category is to use everyone walking down on a core day. This tells you what happens when you run out of stock, as well as when bays are full. This is what cameras in aisles reveal.

You might feel that you can get the same information by simply asking shoppers how they shop; before you set off down this route, please consider:

Our short term working memory retains information for less than 18 seconds... so why ask shoppers about their feelings and behaviour after the event, when they've either forgotten, or have no conscious awareness of their decision making process anyway?

Words themselves represent only 7% of human to human communication. So why rely solely on the words shoppers use when their actions can tell you what they really mean and how they really shopped. 95% of our decision making happens without any conscious awareness.

ACTION: Consider looking at your own category where you underperform as part of a plan to share with your buyer, alongside growing your core stores, to give insight he/she probably won't get anywhere else. You will probably find that, in ROI terms it is a much better investment than buying into omnibus data in terms of change in that group, and, it will probably cost less than you think.

There are a number of companies that offer this. I suggest you start with SBXL. They publish a range of benchmarks as well as an excellent White Paper on selecting and using price points (also in the Dropbox resource mentioned at the beginning of this book).

How do you develop change here?

There are two places where change can be made that will develop improvements to your sales:

Centrally

Here, the objective is to trade extra insight into where you feel the facing can be improved and also your own core stores' data; and trade for additional listings in your core, as well as additional stores.

Locally

As you can see from the research above, store managers in most groups have substantial leeway in what they can achieve, all of which can offer a cost-effective ROI in terms of immediate and long term growth.

Communication with stores needs to focus on benefits for the store, and needs to be absolutely clear as to the action required, which needs to be within the limits of the manager's authority within the group. Communication can be carried out in a variety of ways: mail, telephone, e-mail and lastly, in person. The latter area needs to be handled carefully as a consequence of the risk of unknown quantities when conveying the message. People in the field are great if you need to move objects, but as with communication to shoppers, a mixture of targeted direct media is more effective than a single medium.

Importantly, of course, any change should be monitored with the use of store by store data. In terms of ROI, of all the communication options, personal visits are by far the most expensive and you could stack three or more alternative contacts to reach the same level.

Remember, regularity of contact is as important for your store and store manager market as it is for your shopper and consumer.

The most important stores to contact, and keep in contact with, are your core stores. How to locate these and the key messages for them will be discussed in the next chapter.

Chapter 5

Your Core, How to find it, and Exploit it

There are two quite distinct elements to what is core to your brand.

- The first is the brand values that the consumer and shopper hold for your brand.

- The second is how this plays out at retail across the country.

The two are, of course, inextricably linked, and often the place that you end up is not where you intended to be in the first place.

The decision you then have to take is whether or not you persevere with the original positioning, or understand and accept where you end up.

A couple of examples. My company, Storecheck, understands who buys a product by looking at stores that over-perform against their peers, and have a much greater element of a defined ACORN classification in their catchment area. Here are two scenarios:

- The first: a major chewing gum manufacturer launched a range of mouth freshening strips targeted particularly at young people out on a date, looking for instant fresh breath. They actually gained a second peak from the over 50's. These people also wanted fresh breath, but perhaps had dental issues that made chewing gum impossible.

- The second: a manufacturer of nuts, grains and a number of other healthy eating products. For most of their range they appealed to Educated Urbanites (typical early adopters) and other high income categories. They also had a bulge with Asian communities which is almost unknown in the typical health industry area (except perhaps for fruit drinks). To understand this you only have to look at the range of dried fruit, seeds and nuts stocked in the average Asian local store.

In both cases, the brands were unaware of the additional markets they were reaching.

Sitting in your office, it can be hard to appreciate that people don't toe your party line. It does remind me slightly of the army saying: "no plan survives contact with the enemy" (von Moltke). Basically, if you want to continue to win, you need to be in touch with your market at all times.

A basic war chest would have in it two key facts;

1. Why people buy you.

2. Where people buy you.

1. Why people buy you

Back a long time ago, when instant coffee was new, Mason Haire, a psychologist, prepared two shopping lists. These were identical, except for the fact that one contained ground coffee, and the other, instant coffee.

He then asked subjects to characterise the two lists;

- 48% of people viewed the sort of person who would buy the instant coffee as lazy, and only 4% of the ground coffee users.

- 48% of people viewed the instant coffee user as failing to plan household purchases well, and only 12% of the ground users.

People like you and me generalise all the time as a way of allowing us to make sense of the world around us. Lazy is not necessarily pejorative, of course, and knowing this, you could easily define a campaign that placed instant coffee as part of the lunch break, the fastest way to getting your feet up.

If you actually want to build on the positives in what people think about you, you first want to find out what they are.

One of the besetting issues with market research is interviewer bias. If you ask someone in the street what they think of an issue, their response will, inevitably, be coloured by the way that you approach them and the way that you phrase the question. An example of the latter issue would be, "Have you quit beating your wife lately?" A question for which there is no non-incriminating answer.

Market research needed to go to great lengths with techniques designed to eliminate these effects.

The engram is all about the non-prompted beliefs held about a brand by the consumers/shoppers, and in the era of social networks it is relatively easy to discover what people say about you. In fact any brand worth its salt will already be keeping tabs on this. In particular for the bad news.

From this web activity, the skilled data miner can pull out the key phrases, as well as the demographics of the people who are using them, and whether the attributes are positive or negative. The output bears a startling resemblance to the profile of a brand which cost many thousands of pounds to develop.

The original was called the engram, the set of descriptors that people bring to mind when they think about your product. You will see in the "Thrill of the Deal" that reinforcing or using elements of this engram in promotions is vital for getting success.

In the past, getting to this would have been a really expensive, and time consuming job. In part this is because of the limitations of early research. You had to poll a number of people for descriptions that you knew nothing about, and then pull them together into a mind map. Getting what is, in effect, quantitative data from a qualitative process just has to be expensive.

Trawling the internet is being evaluated by many companies, including IBM. In a study where 300 people had their Twitter profiles processed by the IBM software and also took psychometric surveys, the results were "highly correlated more than 80 percent of the time", Michelle Zhou, leader of the User Systems and Experience Research Group at IBM's Almaden Research Center in California reported.

SpectrumInsight conducted a blind trial against an existing engram (7UP) and found this to be both very accurate, and offering extremely good value for money. This resultant BrandGram 7UP case study is available in the Dropbox. (The engram name has been somewhat monopolised of late by Dianetics).

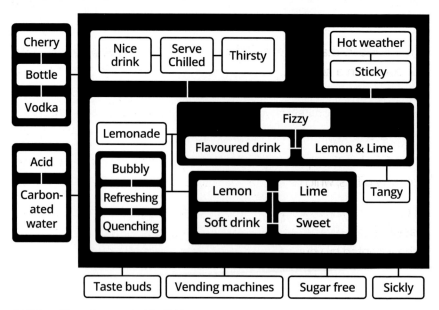

7-UP BrandGram SpectrumInsight 2013

Understanding what people see in your brand is important as it needs to be utilised whenever you plan to promote or redesign. The most important descriptor marking out 7UP is that people believe it is tangy, a drink with a bit of an edge. As you go further out, you find descriptors that are less important, but still relevant.

ACTION: Develop a BrandGram for your product.

You can, of course, develop easily, and inexpensively, BrandGrams for your competition, to see exactly which aspects are uniquely your own.

Using your BrandGram

There are distant options on the BrandGram that could be reinforced, such as the link to mixer, in particular with the new cherry flavour; here the tangy taste belief might lead to a range of new drinks that reinforce additional usage and the core belief.

If you decided that you could extend tangy into a word like edgy, then you could run a series of promotions designed to give people the edge. The edge on holiday (remember the warm weather link), or even in hot weather, using free samples on the tube in London when the refreshing/ quenching element is right to the fore.

If you felt that the appropriate theme might be tasty, you could extend into tasty offers, which might range widely.

All of the above are designed to allow you to consider brand promotions that will extend your image in appropriate ways, and are much more likely to be accepted by your target market.

2. Where people buy you

People with high levels of disposable income tend to prefer Waitrose to Asda:

- In part, because they can afford to;

- In part, because Waitrose is located where they are;

- In part, because shopping at Waitrose is part of how they would define themselves.

Whichever store they choose, there is a distinction between a shopper and a consumer. On one level, it is simply that the shopper does the paying and is a gatekeeper for everyone else. Of course, they are very often also the consumer. It is, though, their behaviour as a shopper that is most important to us, buying perhaps for a number of other people.

Core stores are those where a greater proportion of your own core shoppers live than the average. This means, in the average day, more people who buy, want to buy, or might want to buy, walk through the door.

Typical Core Stores	Sell more from the same space
	Can often run out at peak times
	Promotionally can deliver many times the average uplift
	Are a high proportion of your total sales for their number-even higher on promotion
Non Core Stores	Sell average or less from the space
	Few issues typically with running out
	Promotionally, average or worse performers; some may hardly move
	Are a low proportion of your total sales

How do you spot core stores?

The best way to do this is to find stores that sell more overall vs their peer stores. You can get these stores from dunnhumby for Tesco, Aimia (Nectar) for Sainsbury (if you ask the right questions) or Retail Vital Statistics (retailvitalstatistics.com) for all the key multiples. You could get a handle on your most obvious core stores by looking at the two other measures that distinguish them. The fact that they can run out, which you will have to establish in store, or the promotion uplift, which you can get from epos data.

Under "What Price Success" (Chapter 6), I outline a process using the epos data that you get from retailers for spotting uplifts looking at back data.

Basically you will need to cover a promotion period, and develop a spreadsheet showing the uplift for each store. Here the uplift is defined as the multiple by which sales increase from the week before the activity. Of course, if you are following one promotion with another (such as a "twofer" with a BOGOF) you will need to go back to a previous non-promoted period.

The stores with the greatest uplifts - and here there has to be a substantial difference – are your core stores. They should, of course, be best performers every time, but the limitation of this approach is that a single instance can be impacted by a range of issues including the amount of stock they have at the start. As a result core stores may only perform well 60% (or less) of the time, promotionally. You will get on average a 60% correct store list if you only look at one promotion, but even this will be significantly better than being unaware.

In that chapter you can also see that it is not just the stores with the largest uplifts that matter, but also the extent of that uplift for differing levels of shopper discount.

This process will work well for all the retailers, bar Sainsbury, where you will need to have collected a period of data first.

The objective for core stores, however you identify them, is to get their promotion performance up from 60% to 100%. You will be able to see the potential impact of this, and how to achieve it, in "What Price Success" (Chapter 6). They are the places that off shelf material will work best, as well as secondary siting.

ACTION: Know your core stores and the area they service.

Now let's move on to see what your stores are really like, and how you can get them behind you.

Chapter 6
What Price Success?

Churchill: "Madam, would you sleep with me for five million pounds?"

Socialite: "My goodness, Mr. Churchill ... Well, I suppose ... we would have to discuss terms, of course ... "

Churchill: "Would you sleep with me for five pounds?"

Socialite: "Mr. Churchill, what kind of woman do you think I am?!"

Churchill: "Madam, we've already established that. Now we are haggling about the price."

Price, of course, is an essential element of any sale. Theoretically, if you pay more, you will get more. Whether of course this is true for you will often depend on the value you put on the image of a brand rather than just whether the product will do the basic job you need.

Companies specialise in evaluating this as it now appears on the balance sheet of many companies. It represents the ability to get more from a collection of ingredients than anyone else.

The easy way to make any sale is, of course, to simply reduce the price.

Companies wanting to sell more product use this unmercifully, and it's not just the brands. Retailers push to achieve lower prices since for many of them it is their core USP.

Increasingly brands are not sure that retailers know what they are doing. A survey by Ebiquity for The Grocer in 2012 commented: "No brand can afford to walk away from fairly extensive promotional activity for long. The challenge remains balancing the short-term needs of volume growth with the long-term needs of the business. Focusing on promotional efficiency is the best way of managing this challenge."

IRI (FMCG in Europe 2013 - FMCG Industry at the tipping point) say that currently the cost of promotions to the UK packaged goods industry is £13 Billion. In 2012, when the Ebiquity research was carried out, 68% of companies said that more than 40% of their output was sold on discount - a doubling from 2009. Importantly, 39% said that more than 60% was sold at a discount - an effective trebling of the position.

Ebiquity also asked Sales and Marketing people about their view of the value of price promotions.

41% of sales respondents believe that promotions have a positive impact in driving trial and long-term base sales; only 14% of marketers share this view.

There are (Ebiquity say) a few instances where they have seen this to be true, but these are rare. The vast majority of promotional activity has little long-term impact (positive or negative) on the underlying health of brands.

Promotional activity should be judged on merit, on its ability to deliver the organisation's profit and volume objectives and not on hard-to-quantify, "consumer/shopper" judgements, they say.

The shopper now demands value and service

17% of shoppers are "not satisfied" with the frequency that promoted products are in stock when they want to buy them (IGD Shoppertrack survey). The Grocer found that availability was 92.9% which offers a major opportunity in a £120 billion market.

A significant proportion of shoppers also say that when they are frustrated in trying to buy a product on offer they are left with a bias against the product and feel forced to trial the competition. Consequently, they may leave a brand permanently.

Some previous research has already been done in this area, by the IGD in 2003. Clearly the impact will be different depending on the product area. As an example, a staple product with no alternative (such as bread or milk) would have a different profile from a more discretionary product.

For an average product the IGD found that:

- 37% of shoppers would go to another store.

- 6% would not buy at all;
  - leading to a loss of 43% of intended purchases for retailers.

- 19% of shoppers would switch to a rival brand;
  - when added to the 6% who would not buy at all this leads to a loss of 25% of intended purchases for manufacturers.

More recently a study commissioned by SCALA Consulting, the supply chain consultants, in 2009 found almost half of those questioned said they would only tolerate products being out of stock two or three times before switching to another supermarket. Nearly half of those quizzed said that if they couldn't find their favourite brand they would simply buy an alternative. This represents a retrograde step from 2003 for brands.

Yet many brands seem unconcerned. SCALA Consulting also commissioned a survey of some of the biggest global brands and over a quarter of those questioned (26%) – representing a cross section from the FMCG and grocery sector - did not view on shelf availability as a key success factor for their company. What is more, a third (33%) didn't have on shelf availability as a key business objective.

In 2009 a survey updating the IGD figures found that if products are out of stock two or three times this lead to nearly 50% switching to another supermarket and 50% buying an alternative brand.

Yes, it's all doom and gloom

But that does not mean there are not opportunities to profit from being that little bit smarter than the rest. Firstly, it is important to accept that many companies want to wind back the clock. It will, though, be hard to do this, since most companies, and retailers, need the volume, and promotions are a part of the support package that stores expect.

First objective is properly managed price promotions

The Ebiquity report asked companies what their major promotion management challenges were. They said it was:

- Developing clear objectives (71%)

- Lack of post evaluation (61%)

- Systems or data integration (45%)

- Volume focus (36%)

- Lack of pre-evaluation (23%)

Companies also felt that their challenges split into two areas:

1. Hard promotion objectives – headed by securing in-store display, and then, right at the bottom, availability.

2. Academic objectives such as intensity of competition increased funding demands, deepening discounts and decreasing ROI.

These latter points are academic, in the sense that the academic objectives are entirely unrelated to making a success of price promotions, they are a part of either the strategic environment or of the way you actually manage your promotions.

So, what can you impact?

The Rumsfeld Effect in detail – store availability and store support

There seems to be a general belief that stores and their management actually stand in the way of the brand and the store systems, and that store systems are the bees knees.

If you actually believe this then there is very little point in reading on. Much of what can be achieved needs to be managed down to local level. Store managers can be great enablers if you have a message that is relevant to them, and to their personal success. If your brand is important to their shoppers, then it is also important to their success.

It is interesting that companies placed lack of pre-evaluation at the very end of their list of challenges, when you would have thought that the very first place you would start is with a plan.

They also placed post-evaluation much higher up. Naturally, understand the one and you deliver on the other. However, you do not have to know everything. Remember that really important question concerning bear hunting?

How fast do you have to run to get away from an angry bear?

The answer, of course, is just a little bit faster than the slowest member of the party.

Many people look at a problem and think that they need to know all about it. When actually all they need to know is more than their competitors.

Supply systems are exactly as good as the programs they run, the assumptions they have built in, and the people pressing the buttons.

All of which means that they are actually the weak point in your promotions strategy.

The most important availability is Day 1 of the promotion in the store. Peak demand is Weekend 1 of any promotion, since it is the first time everyone, including the store staff, has seen it. Typically, though, peak supply will be the LAST week.

Retail stores with an adequate stock level who are aware of the importance of your brand to their store will allocate additional space.

There are therefore three imperatives if you want core store support so they can maximise their customer support and your sales:

1. Set the right discount levels

2. Get the right level of product into each store and not in the depot

3. Make sure that your core stores know the mutual importance of your brand to their customers

The theory behind pricing and shopper impact

SBXL (Shopper Behaviour Xplained) have spent some years identifying the key measures that cause shoppers to track through the major stages in an in-store purchase. Stages are identified as:

1. Stopping from moving down the aisle

2. Visiting the shelf, looking closer

3. Evaluating, picking up and looking at a product or products

4. Buying

_____

They do this with the use of CCTV cameras covering the aisle, tracking the way that individual shoppers move, in a number of categories, on many occasions. Using identical measures they are then able to see the difference when the environment changes.

They have used a very large number of shoppers in 11 key categories, across the 3 major supermarkets in the UK. In doing this, they have been able to distinguish some real differences in the way that shoppers behave to certain types of offer prices.

 Their research highlights the fact that large changes in sales are built on moving relatively few people from their normal behaviour, when you compare pre- with post- change. They give you the following guidelines as to what works in stores:

1. Promoted products accounted for only 4 percentage points more of product sales than they had share of shelf.

2. Special offers are shopped more after something else has been looked at. If sufficiently interesting then shoppers will switch to them: secondary choice, more than primary visibility.

3. When 37% of products on shelf are promoted, shoppers are 10% more likely to buy one of them. (Promoting when the brand leaders promote could be a winning strategy).

4. At a more detailed level, once they show an interest in a product, shoppers are five times more likely to buy it if it is on promotion.

5. Asda and Sainsbury's shoppers are more likely to buy after evaluating if the product is on offer; Tesco shoppers on the other hand are less likely.

6. The best way to stop shoppers in their tracks is to present them with a BOGOF: this type of promotional mechanic was more than twice as effective as any of the others measured.

7. In terms of getting shoppers to actively browse a product, then the clear winner again is the BOGOF.

8. When it comes to getting shoppers to evaluate a product, once again, BOGOF was the most effective.

9. BOGOF was the best way to drive sales, achieving a sales rating almost three times that of an un-promoted alternative.

10. A 'save' offer that ends on some 'random pence' is much less effective at all levels compared to finishing it with either a round pound or a round '50p'.

11. When it comes to Multibuys, the round pound ending is actually the least effective pence treatment for the offer.

12. When looking at all offer types and in particular the pence of the price point, the round 50p is the most effective tool, by some margin.

13. Rounder price points are generally more effective on promotions, and overall round pound and round 50p perform very similarly.

Planning your promotions properly

There are two really important factors to be aware of when you are evaluating past promotions to plan for the next:

1. There is often not a straight line relationship between levels of discount and sales uplift. This means that there will be a sweet spot where you can maximise your return.

2. To maximise the performance of your core, stores need at least a normal week's sales in stock in the store on Day 1 to cope with the first weekend. But this could rise to as much as 2/3 week's normal sales in stock, on the floor, for many brands. Not in the warehouse. Demand ramps up immediately.

3. Core stores, those with the greatest number of the right kind of people have a much greater uplift potential and need comparatively more stock. Core stores might be 20% of stores but 50% of business normally, 60% PLUS promotionally. Manage these first and foremost.

Ideally you should build a chart that looks like this. It shows the uplift you get from core stores (good performers) vs the rest. The "blob" size is driven by the stock cover, the number of times more than pre-sales that needs to be in the store day one. The chart below is a summary of around 100 products from different companies. It will not be yours.

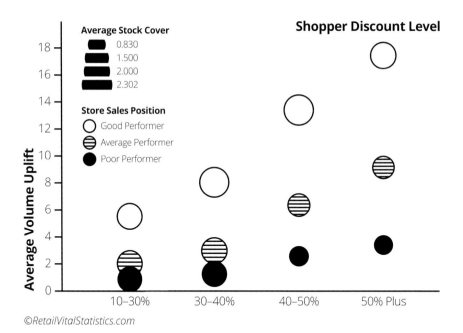

©RetailVitalStatistics.com

Uplifts tend to be much higher in Asda and Morrisons than they are in Tesco and Sainsbury.

To identify uplift from your core stores, you need to go back over a few promotions to see this. Never rely on what you sold last time in that store, since if supply chain let you down then, the repercussions will continue into the future.

Here you will need to build a spreadsheet or database of all stores including the week before, and chart the results that you achieved by type of offer from the week before.

Core stores, whatever their size, will perform much better overall and need your help. In the above chart drawn from real life, you can see that a core store should have an 18 times uplift. An average store, eight times, while a poor store a mere three. Core stores are not just the larger stores. In fact some larger stores may actually be poor performers.

If you work with just the largest stores possibly over half of your investment will be substantially wasted on stores with little hope of growth.

If you understand what these stores can do, and what they need, then you can find a way to give it to them. This can be by discussion with supply chain centrally, or at store level. Remember that to get zynergy from this activity you need to tell the stores what you are doing. It would also help if you asked them what else they needed!

What can you gain?

Well there have been a number of improved promotion events managed by Storecheck, using these criteria. They have in house a client quote saying that they doubled sales in Asda, another **adding £100,000 to Tesco sales in just 20 core stores** at no cost. In both cases these were managed by central allocation alone.

The benefit that can be gained by adding in POP and additional store communication can be even greater than this.

Promoting price promotions to customers

Hey, you know you have to do them, you want to make more money, and have fewer periods when you are discounted. You have developed your packs so you actually make money promotionally. The obvious solution is to make more of the promotions that you do have. If you look at Chapter 7 "In Place of Price" you will see how keen people are to share and receive good news. There is little more exciting than a good deal. So collect e-mail addresses, use social media, and let them know.

Research with SpectrumInsight with one client shows that the more promotions there were in the category, the greater the brand uplifts actually were. This might be counter-intuitive if you were not aware that one of the measures they tracked to uncover the strength of the offer was the amount that people discussed it on the web. The more popular the more word of voice advertises it.

Don't be shy, tell people what you are doing. They will be grateful, and you will be better off.

Build e-mail databases of your users (see how to do this in other chapters) and regularly tell them where they can buy you at a discount. They may not take advantage, but will tell their friends, and will be grateful you thought about them.

Promoting price promotions to stores

You will recall that I suggested you start by researching your core stores, and finding out if they know that your brands are important to them. You need one piece of information they do not have. That is, a view of what they should sell (the uplift multiple) against what they were selling before.

You also need a second piece of information. The amount of stock they should have. This information could be used centrally to generate additional allocations, or locally, to get an appropriate increase in shelf max or cube (there are other measures in use by various retailers), depending on how compliant central stock control is. **Win.**

If you have collected from your customers the exact store they shop in, you can also tell that store manager you are driving people in.

Win Win – Ching Ching

ACTION: Understand the promotion performance parameters of your brands and the core store impact. Download the "In Place of Price" White Paper from the Dropbox which gives you suggestions from experts as to improved retailer presentations, and suggestions on how to manage your promotion reporting and planning.

Best practice discount management

There are a number of organisations offering advice on how to manage a relationship with a retailer better. One of these is Simon-Kucher. They are international experts in the area of pricing. Alongside these are Ebiquity, who I have quoted from before and who run The Grocer research into the whole area of discounting. For additional information here, pull down a copy of "In Place of Price" from the Dropbox. You can also look at Gus Ormond presenting on how to manage price discounting in a video on YouTube: *http://www.youtube.com/watch?v=r2sUFOWXPj0*

There is a great deal more in the White Paper, "In Place of Price" that this section only touches on (available to download from the website). Initially setting up a process to manage price discounts is absolutely vital. I have therefore included the Simon-Kucher recommendations, as they are very similar to others, and there is good documentation available.

They identify five key steps to realising the potential value of price discounting:

1. Develop a promotional strategy that gives you the right framework to build your calendar.

2. Identify which packs and promotions work best for your brands.

3. Create a strong calendar planning process that allows you to maximise your profits.

4. Look at promotions not only from an internal perspective, but also from a retailer and category perspective.

5. Put in place the infrastructure to sustain promotional management.

Developing strong promotional management takes time, but each step should deliver profit upsides. The more expertise you develop the more value you can realise; even a pilot project can help you to start reaping the benefits. The hardest part is often making the first step.

1. Setting the promotional strategy

In many cases promotional strategy is owned by a wide range of stakeholders: senior management, sales, marketing, supply chain, finance to name just the obvious candidates. It's not unusual to have multiple objectives (e.g. drive trial, secure listings, hit sales targets and drive incremental profit) all influencing the same promotional calendar. In this situation the sales team has the near impossible task of trying to reconcile all these conflicting needs and still hit their targets.

Having a clear promotional strategy is the key foundation to building the "right" calendar. In the real world this involves making trade-offs and prioritising some objectives over others. The key stages are:

1. Understand the objectives of different stakeholders

2. Score these objectives in a quantitative way

3. Bring the stakeholders together to agree the priorities and make the trade-offs

4. Stress-test the output against the broader corporate strategy.

Equally it's important to understand how your brands react to promotions. For example is your brand expandable (i.e. if shoppers buy more on promotion do they consume more or do consumers simply load the pantry)? How substitutable is your product (e.g. do you steal from other categories when you promote)? What is the relative size and penetration of your brand? Answering these questions will help determine what type of promotions you should run. For example if your category is not highly expandable single pack deals may be more attractive than multi-buy promotions.

With a clear context and strategy you can determine the objectives and key performance indicators for your promotions.

2. Identifying the right promotional mechanics

Different promotional mechanics have an enormous impact on the uplift and incremental profit a promotion generates. Consumers will react very differently to the same price discount, depending on how it is presented. For a product with an everyday price of £1.49 a Half Price promotion can perform far more strongly than a £0.74 pricedown on some products. Equally, on a different product a 74p price point may appear very attractive. Simply plotting percent discount or absolute promoted price and expecting consumer demand to react in a strictly mathematical way will lead to sub-optimal decision-making. Using the analytic process described earlier in the chapter, it is easy to pull out the best performing level.

There is, again as stressed earlier, no substitute for post-auditing different promotions over a 1-2 year timeframe. Many companies have the base data already, and this database of promotions enables you to identify which promotion types perform for you, as well as enabling you to predict how new untried promotional mechanics may perform. The process of tracking back recommended earlier in this chapter is a necessary precursor to this process.

3. Building the right promotional calendar

A good promotional calendar is not just a piece of paper with a list of promotions; it's the process to turn a strategy and a list of mechanics into an executable plan. A promotional calendar should encompass all the commercial activity within a particular retailer and work across retailers and channels. Price discounting is not the only option, as you have seen above, and a good calendar should contain a variety of tactics. These are discussed in the next chapter "In Place of Price".

The role of the calendar is to determine the pattern of promotional activity (frequency, depth, number of brands, etc.). This depends on the nature of the brand and the strategy you have adopted. Calendar planning should also cover all the key retailers and channels. One of the most important objectives of the process is to ensure that promotions in one account or channel do not have a negative cross-read impact in others.

Determining the correct discount levels for a brand is often one of the most contentious questions. Retailers will always push for the most attractive possible promotion, and there is often a clear trade-off for suppliers between sales and profit. Simon-Kucher would always advise clients to follow a balanced approach, only proposing deeper promotions where they can do so at a reasonable return. For example in a recent project Simon-Kucher identified that a shallower more frequent promotional strategy would deliver much greater returns for one key brand, than the current less frequent and deeper promotional pattern. The deeper promotions performed strongly on some of their other brands, and retaining these promotions was important in maintaining engagement with the retailer.

A calendar planning process should aim to get ahead of retailer, competitor and supply chain issues. Planning 6-9 months ahead allows time to make trade-offs and also allows time to revise the plan. Things will inevitably change, but it's easier to make snap decisions when a framework and strategy already exists.

With a process in place to plan promotions you will begin to develop more informed promotional strategies. As your stock of promotional audits increases, so will your ability to build your calendar to maximise profit.

4. Developing a 360 degree view of promotions

Understanding promotional performance from your own perspective is vital to developing an effective promotional strategy. The ability, though, to analyse promotions from the retailer and category perspective is the key to successfully implementing that strategy. Simon-Kucher hear frequently from clients "We know what the right strategy is, but the big supermarkets won't listen". Simon-Kucher also believes that a promotion strategy should be focused as equally on the stores as on the shopper. They believe that you will not truly know what the right strategy is, unless you know whether it works for your retail partners as well.

The first step is to fully understand the retailer strategy, both at a buyer level, but also at a more senior management level. If your buyer is focussed on margin, you should ensure that the promotions you propose are margin accretive. Similarly if the senior management is focussed on share, your promotional strategy should support this objective.

The second and most simple step is to ensure that all the analysis and planning of promotions that you do includes retailer margin. A good test of your promotional calendar for a subsequent quarter is whether it is margin accretive at a per cent or absolute level vs the prior year. A buyer is much more likely to be receptive to a shallower deal if the margin upside is shared between the retailer and supplier.

The more advanced step is to develop an understanding of how your promotions impact the category. A promotion which has a low level of cannibalisation of your products may drive little true incrementality for the category, and be unattractive to a retailer. Shopper panel data and consumer surveys can often give a good idea of how much volume is stolen from within the category. Understanding how your promotions perform versus the competition can often be the most insightful data for a retailer, and proposing a calendar that balances retailers and suppliers profit is a powerful win-win.

Adding some weight to the need for a category view is research from William P. Putsis, Jr. in the US. While this paper was produced in 1998, it covered a broad range, and represents a factual base from which to work (see the Dropbox). In this paper, two broad factors (category characteristics and competitive interactions) were identified that underlie the manner in which promotions can increase category revenue.

Contrasting with previous research suggesting that the impact of promotions on category consumption is either a zero sum game or large they found the impact was significant but modest. Further, their research suggests that:

- for the majority of packaged goods, promotions can indeed increase category.

- the impact on category expenditure is generally small, but is significant for a number of categories.

- there is significant variation in the potential for promotions to increase category varying by type of promotion, and the category concerned.

- there are wide differences between "stronger" and "weaker" brands.

The study reported here was limited to food products in the US. The conventional wisdom that advertising and promotion have negligible effect on total category demand in the mid-term seems to have been understated in the case of promotion - at least for the categories studied.

Finally, the study suggests that managers should plan and evaluate promotions in terms of the extent to which they cause category expansion, in addition to brand switching and purchase acceleration considerations.

5. Putting in the infrastructure to sustain promotional management

Getting your promotional calendar right should not be viewed as a one-off project. Managing promotions effectively requires buy-in across your organisation, good quality data and an on-going process to manage calendars. The commercial environment is fluid and a promotional strategy that worked in one quarter, may not be appropriate 12 months later.

That doesn't mean you should go out and invest significant amounts immediately. Kick-starting the process with a study of previous promotions for a specific brand or retailer is a good place to start. The data you gather should give you the evidence you need to justify a larger investment. Executive teams always want to see the money before making a bet on something new and untried in the organisation. Even a limited study can identify optimisation opportunities and you will find many activity advocates based on the outcome.

In order to realise the full upside potential having a dedicated resource is vital. The analysis required is often complex and requires experience. Managing multiple retailers and channels adds complexity and more stakeholders to manage. In addition the individual or team needs to build links across multiple functions (sales, marketing, finance, supply chain, etc.). Companies, of course, could either recruit this resource, or buy in the experience from external companies.

The return on investment for a promotions team is frequently very high, as even small changes to promotional calendars can generate significant profit impact.

This approach is designed to turn promotions from being a challenge and a drain on P&L to a strategic lever that enables you to hit your objectives.

Chapter 7
In Place of Price

It is, of course, easy to set up the next price discount. All you have to do is decide how deep. The fact that volume can be bought so easily is, of course, the reason why it became so popular. Many companies now complain that it has become an enormous tail wagging an increasingly small dog.

A discount is exciting for the shopper. Mintel report that "seven in ten say they like the thrill of getting a bargain". In fact, many people are so excited that they go out of their way to share this with their friends on web sites such as www.hotukdeals.com. The fact that they do this can actually be used to find out which of all of the many offers that are available are the most engaging.

Actually, many companies do not know that shoppers say they are much keener to report good news than bad. People like to share positive experiences, even though marketers think their major motivation is to deliver negative reviews.

Motivation to write reviews	Consumer view	Marketer view of consumer	GAP
Never write reviews	42%	29%	-30.95%
To share positive and negative experiences	32%	17%	-46.88%
To take part in competition or prize draw	13%	15%	15.38%
Competition	15%	16%	6.67%
To share positive experience	10%	16%	60.00%
To share negative experience	4%	23%	475.00%
	22%	**19%**	**-16.96%**

IPM fast.MAP Marketing Gap 2013

In whatever form, UK shoppers want to get a "thrill" out of their shopping, and share it. The increasing flight to discounting does deliver a thrill as a cheap and cheerful way of getting volume out of the door of the factory.

But this thrill can be gained in more than one way as is exemplified by research carried out by the IPM together with iMotions in 2010. This showed that a good on-pack promotion actually gave a response in the eye that was comparable to that of low grade pornography. This message made headlines around the world – type "Colin Harper" and "porn" into your browser. (See "In Place of Price" IPM Publication for details).

Bargain hunting has become ingrained among Britons with more than half buying certain products/brands only when they were on promotion. In this case promotional activity has moved from being a means of generating interest, to actually discouraging purchase outside of promotional periods.

Alongside the trend to look for the lowest possible price comes the increased use of money off vouchers and coupons, as well as the continuing use of loyalty points. All of this re-emphasises that promotion techniques are all-pervasive. Significantly less than 10% of people reported that they used no promotion techniques at all.

Promotions typically taken advantage of	%
Multibuys	72
Money off e.g. save 30p	65
Extra FREE	46
Loyalty points	41
Coupons/Vouchers	31
Free sample	27
All inclusive meal deals	17
Free gift with purchase	12
Buy now get discount later	7
On pack competitions	4
Other	1
Don't use	4

Mintel "Attitudes towards Pricing and Promotions in Food and Drink (2013)"

Demographic Divergence

Further enhancing this trend, growth in lower socio economic areas will impact more in the future. C1 socio economic groups - expected to account for more than 25% of the UK population by 2019 suggests that everyday low pricing will continue to resonate. Consumers in this category are more likely on average to say that they prefer low prices across the store to getting specific products on promotion.

Alongside this "flight to the bottom" some people continue to do well.

Consumers in the AB economic group - forecast to see growth of 3.5% over the same period – are significantly more likely on average to say that they buy what they want regardless of price, and that quality is more important than price. In terms of appropriate techniques for this very important category, the fast.MAP (Marketing Gap 2011) research showed that these upmarket people were much more likely to have a basket prompted by more creative promotion techniques.

While discounts, therefore, are a promotion technique, they are by no means the only one available. The whole principle behind a promotion is to offer a reward to get instant, or at least more rapid purchasing. Many techniques offer better VFM than discounting, where you actually lose margin on every product you sell.

A reward does not have to be money; it can be as little as re-assurance. In the convenience trade, price-marked packs have an edge on plain ones. Meanwhile, The Grocer reported that the successful launch of the Asda pound range meant that prices went UP as well as down.

Promotions are designed to change behaviour. They are a very important element of turning a warm body in front of a product into a sale. They can also serve many functions for an organisation or brand. Our key focus here is how best to convert a shopper to a purchaser.

Avoiding The Rumsfeld Effect in promotions

First and foremost it is important to understand that for many people, an offer of a benefit can be nearly as strong as the benefit itself. "Which" magazine in the UK reported that only 8% of people actually claimed an offer made to them in any form. Obviously 92% of people are quite happy with the offer alone.

So why don't more people use other promotion techniques to build the brand? They are designed to give sales this year working with brand values, and not against them.

A price discount is, in effect, a gift with purchase. You could, though, deliver the same gift, or even more: get £1 back (as opposed to 50p off now) if people send away for it. The result is a sales increase for a fraction of the cost of a discount.

Before starting we need to avoid making mistakes by learning a little more about the reaction of shoppers to various types of promotion activity.

Question	Consumer view	Marketer view of consumer	GAP
I like to buy a brand on promotion	71.00%	38.00%	-46.48%
I like to buy new brands I have not seen before	42.00%	23.00%	-45.24%
I like to buy the same brands each time	39.00%	30.00%	-23.08%
I like to buy on the lowest price regardless of brand	38.00%	31.00%	-18.42%
I like to buy the same brands even if there is a cheaper alternative	33.00%	25.00%	-24.24%
I like to buy the same brands even if there is a promotion on other brands	30.00%	24.00%	-20.00%
Average	**42.17%**	**28.50%**	**-32.41%**

IPM fast.MAP Marketing Gap 2013

Marketers consistently underestimate the drive for a little bit of excitement in the shop, which is why people look for something new, at the same time as they look for a deal. Look at Chapter 9 on adding NEW signage to a pack to see that effect in action.

It is also worth noting that roughly the same percentage of respondents claim to be loyal to brand, as claim to buy at the lowest price regardless of brand.

Marketers, though, are even worse when they look at the relative impacts of a promotional message on behaviour.

How likely are you to switch to an alternative product if offered this promotion?	Consumer view	Marketer view of consumer	GAP
Buy one get one free	85%	42%	-50.59%
Lower price by more than 10%	82%	33%	-59.76%
Lower price by up to 10%	68%	24%	-64.71%
Competition	41%	15%	-63.41%
Free prize Draw	40%	16%	-60.00%
Average	**63%**	**26%**	**-58.86%**

IPM fast.MAP Marketing Gap 2013

Marketers underestimate the impact on the consumer of anything that promises to offer interest in the store. This is common to all kinds of promotion activity, although varying by degree.

Where marketers tend to over-estimate the impact of techniques is in the area of sampling. Here, of course, there are two ways of viewing this. Unlike promotions, where you cannot avoid them, it can be easy to miss sampling. In that regard it is probable that marketers actually over-estimate the reach rather than the impact of sampling. Whatever the reason, targeted sampling at the home OR sampling near the POP are reported as being most influential in trialling a new product.

What is clear is that only 56% of the sample said that they have not bought a product for the first time after a trial. So if your sampling is inexpensive enough, there is a ready market out there waiting to try.

Buy product for the first time after trial	Consumer view	Marketer view of consumer	GAP
No, have not bought	56%	22%	-60.71%
Postal sample	19%	20%	5.26%
Sample asked for online	19%	20%	5.26%
In and around stores	15%	21%	40.00%
At friends, relatives or colleagues	10%	16%	60.00%
An event	7%	21%	200.00%
Street, shopping centre, or in the community	7%	16%	128.57%
Average	**24%**	**20%**	**-16.81%**

IPM fast.MAP Marketing Gap 2013

Marketers are very poor judges of what consumers report they have done.

Why use non-discount promotions?

£13 Billion is spent on discounting, and in the current market conditions you cannot rely on people beating a path to your door (website, shelf space...) just because you are there. Messaging, as you will see, also stacks. So sampling and discounting will stack. On-pack and discounting will stack.

Stacking is very important indeed. In "Models of Marketing Effectiveness" the IPA reported that "Advertising coupled with a sales conversion channel such as direct marketing or sales promotion is the most effective combination to drive hard business success".

There is every reason to include promotions – as opposed to discounts – as an integral part of your plan. In fact, if you manage your price discounts properly, and maximise your returns, you would be well advised to take some investment from here, and focus on the people walking down the aisle who are interested in other aspects of your brand than simply the price.

Used promotions in last 12 months	Consumer
Reward or loyalty schemes	58%
Printed coupon by post	48%
Printing coupon from internet	45%
Pack coupon	43%
Printed coupon from elsewhere	40%
Free prize draws	40%
Printed coupon through the door	37%
Prize promotions where you enter a competition	36%
Coupon website such as Groupon	20%
Gift with purchase or enquiry	15%
Mobile phone coupon	10%
None of the above	10%
	34%

IPM fast.MAP Marketing Gap 2013

What a choice there is too. The IPM have a White Paper – "Sustainable Promotions" – that is also available in the Dropbox. This lists the many types that are available.

Of course, in this book, my sole interest is to suggest that you stack incentives that will either appear in the core store as a matter of course, or can be economically targeted around the core store area. This is to be able to deliver the very best affordable growth for the company and the retailer.

From the point of view of the company, nothing persuades like success, and funnily enough, it's the same with the group buyers too.

Successful non-price promotions

1. Tailoring the incentive to the objective.

2. Tapping into the customers psyche immediately with the creative.

Taking these in order:

1. Tailoring the incentive to the objective:

It is possible, and very common, to over-incentivise people. This is particularly the case with 'cash' rewards. Cash incentives can be used right across the company from sales through to HR, where changed behaviour or improved performance can attract sometimes vast rewards (as witnessed with banker's bonuses). For the target market a downloaded iTune may have a much greater perceived value than a retail discount.

'Slippage' (the difference between the number of people that buy a product to take advantage of an offer and the number that actually do so) has the potential to magnify the promotional budget even further. With an 'instant win' promotion, only a small percentage of the prizes available are claimed, so the potential prize fund can be enormous and protected by insurance. With a price promotion, every single purchase costs money.

Often when evaluating such promotions the cost and the benefit are not even discussed. In the case of the bankers it is "a price you have to pay to recruit" (we are told). In the case of price discounts at supermarkets a similar argument is also deployed – "it's just the cost of doing business".

All incentives must have a purpose or an objective that can be questioned and evaluated. Every company ought to know what options exist for alternate means of achieving that objective.

Slippage definitely pays the promoter. VCG Promorisk, who measure and manage risk for clients, give some examples here of how you get significantly lower % redemptions for different types of promotions.

Promotion type	Redemption Range
Coupon (£2.00 item with £0.50p coupon)	
Doordrop	2 – 4%
On-pack (coupon off same product)	6 – 10%
Download online coupon	40% - 50%
Free holiday (Family Holiday Abroad)	
Prize draw via direct mail / doordrop	1 – 1.5%
Prize draw via on-pack	2 – 5%
Prize draw via press	0.5 – 1.5%
Instant win via on-pack (Cash & free product)	1.5% – 15%
Collector scheme via on-pack (Token collector for themed merchandise)	3% – 10%

VCG Promorisk 2013

One advantage of having companies specialising in the area of risk management is that if you have a project you can't see above, you contact them, and they will give you an estimate of risk, and quote you a fixed price for managing the project for you. This offers the opportunity to take some of the risk out of non-price activity.

You can find their details in the contacts section at the back.

2. Tapping into the customer's current psyche and Communicating the benefit;

Recently, in the UK, £1 has taken up the role that 99p used to have as a key price point. Just advertising that you sell a product at £1 seems to guarantee that it is a good deal, as Asda demonstrated when they launched their '£1 range', increasing some products in price to get there. Similarly a recent entry for the IPM (then ISP) Awards played on the "Scrappage Scheme" to promote the window replacement market. Would customers have responded to the approach so fast if the Government had not just spent a fortune elevating it to the zeitgeist?

Communication should be designed to reach a customer as rapidly and effectively as possible. A recent IPSOS Mori report drawn from many markets, and thousands of adverts, nominated the creative approach as the one key element in the success of a campaign. It is vital to recognise here that you have at most seconds to get someone's attention, so this area cannot be underestimated. It should be clear then that the most important part of any promotion is the communication - and not necessarily just the value, since value is in the eye of the beholder.

Considering that the longer term might lead, for example, to offering a free branded item which may be more expensive than a cash discount, if it has 'play value' for children it could offer substantial additional advertising to the target market.

Promotions as exciting as porn?

Utilising the BrandGram for impact

The Institute of Promotional Marketing in the UK worked together with iMotions – a radical eye tracking technique that pulls back the interest people have in a visual, as well as simply where people look first. The IPM examined the credentials of a range of award winning promotions for their impact on the shopper. People respond to sights of interest by changing their blink rate, as well as their pupils expanding, both of which are externally measurable. iMotions has validated its approach on a scale of 1-10 where 10 is the most emotional view you could conceive of (extreme distress, or sexuality as an example). In August 2010 the IPM put standard packs and promotions in front of consumers, and measured the impact. The results, from their first release in The Grocer, lead to world wide reporting.

The incentive varied from the very strong, such as FREE, to the weak, such as competitions. A Kingsmill Bread promotion featuring Wallace and Gromit added considerable "eye-appeal" to the pack, in large part as it featured a very relevant film, "A Matter of Loaf and Death". More to the point, the FREE offer of a clockwork toast rack was both novel and very relevant.

The ultimate in "eye candy" promotions belonged to Marmite – not perhaps the brand you would at first have nominated for the honour. But in the eyes of the shopper a reading of 5.8 puts it up there with pictures you would more commonly expect in top shelf magazines. All this was generated by a free offer of a book, associated with the line "Marmite is Perfect" and free gifts of the "Horrid Henry" series of books.

If you look at the BrandGram from Marmite it is easy to see how an emotional message plays so well. The core messaging (darker and closer to the centre) are Toast and Love. Meanwhile it is surrounded by concepts such as Craving, Mum, Bed and Home. Easy to see then that a link with "Horrid Henry" will bring all this emotion to the fore.

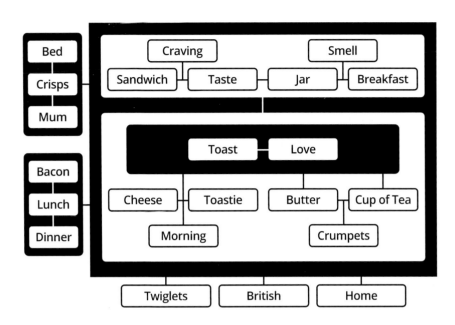

Both the above illustrations of course, stress the simple need for relevance in the promotion message.

Utilising salience

As a further indication of the importance of relevance, and moving away from FMCG, we have the Anglia Windows scrappage scheme. This paralleled a scrappage scheme for cars that received wide publicity, and was Government funded.

There was nothing special about the benefit — basically another way of offering a discount. What was different about this approach is that it tapped into a very top of mind issue in another market, cars. It gave a reason for giving a payback, wholly different from simply discounting the product.

A result of this tight link to customer top of mind, the campaign took the industry by storm, and has been replicated by all the major competitors.

Homeowners received an allowance when they traded in their old windows. This was communicated through DRTV, national press, online, door drops and foot canvassing.

- Against a target of 2,150 leads - £1.7 million worth of business, the campaign delivered 9,867 leads over the target period.

- The campaign peaked with a cost per sale of 12% versus the same period the previous year of 21%.

- Sales rose 126% year on year, and in December despite spend being 11% down on the previous year sales kept coming and were 68% up on the previous year.

If you intend your promotions to compete against simply dropping the price, they have to be relevant at the point at which the shopper sees them.

Get it right, and on pack promotions, rated at number 13 in the list developed by the British Consumer Index, can soar up to number 1.

Plus, if you offer something that seems to be a price offer on pack (such as "Try me Free") this can have a high impact on the shelf browser. Power without the price, since the redemptions are a fraction of the cost of making a similar offer through the medium of discounting. Moreover, on-pack offers tend to target people who can afford to carry on buying at full price afterwards, since, of course, they buy at full price to be able to claim!

Stacking Activity

Bear in mind that the magic media number is three as reported by the IPA (see next chapter). This should be supplemented on the path to purchase, with particular reference to in-store, to six.

While there may well be an instinctive aversion to adding other messaging to a price discount, there is significant evidence that if you manage availability, benefit stacks here too.

Chapter 8

The Long and Winding Road

Outside of stores, but relating to the shopper, there is an increasing number of very effective media you can use for research as well as promotion. As I write this today I see a headline from Morrisons reporting to have increased its number of new and reactivated customers by 150% by targeting postal areas where people shopped with other grocers, using mobile data.

Outside of the store is a fertile ground for reaching prospects, and bringing them in to view and buy. Small area advertising is called hyper-local. A recent report for NESTA estimated this market to be worth up to £2.6 billion a year. £731 million is spent online, of which £23 million is on hyper-local websites. The remainder is spent on local newspapers, posters etc.

This is, by any standards, a large figure, the online section of which is expected to grow to £1.4 billion within 5 years.

Choosing your channel

An insight into what the shoppers feel is the most influential way of getting a new product into their hands is delivered by the British Consumer Index (from the British Population Survey). The types of promotion surveyed, and reported in the table, are both "in-store" and "on the way to the store".

The British Consumer Index is a continual tracking study of the population based on a "population-representative" sample of 13,107 face to face "in home" interviews (aged 15+). The Index constantly monitors a wide range of "Influences to purchase" as part of its continuous tracking of the population.

The latest publication of the data (Q1 2013) shows that more people are influenced by their family and friends than anything else, closely followed by good experience in the past.

Advice from friends and family
Past experience of brand or retailer
In-store sales discounts

HIGH Influence 40% or More

- Offers or vouchers through the door
- Price comparison websites
- Seen on TV
- Email offers vouchers
- Online customer reviews
- Magazine/newspaper reviews
- Internet offers (e.g. Groupon)
- Sales persons advice

LOW influence 10% or Less

- On-pack promotions
- Professional advisor
- Newspaper offers or voucher

- Offers by post
- Leaflets while shopping
- Recommendations on social networks
- Competitions
- Brands on Facebook, Twitter
- Mobile phone offers while shopping
- Celebrity Endorsement
- Prize draws
  - Offers and discounts are far more important than endorsements, competitions and "buzz".
  - Leaflets through the door are far more influential than those handed out while shopping.
  - Mobile is still very much in its infancy and should move up the rankings dramatically.
  - On and offline reviews, both matter equally.
  - TV is still important.
  - "Real World" friends and family carry a lot more weight than 'virtual' friends.

Commenting on the figures, Steve Abbott, Director of The British Consumer Index said; "These figures throw up some interesting dilemmas for marketers. The consumer landscape is, as we all know, changing rapidly to a more digital environment. The problem is that many in the marketing industry are far more advanced in their engagement with the digital world than the population in general. This data provides a 'reality check' which can help bring a better balance to the weighting of marketing spend".

It is, of course, the case that the most important discriminator for the marketer is not necessarily selecting the technique with the most impact. It is selecting those which are most cost-effective in delivering the objective. In that regard, on-pack activity, costing significantly less than discounts, may well offer a perfect match. A combination of an on-pack, supported by a door drop leaflet, with another kind of local media, that could be radio, poster, local press or online.

1 plus 1 equals?

To assess the impact of multilayered messaging, the IPA (Institute of Practitioners in Advertising) have produced a seminal report "New Models of Advertising Integration, from Segmentation to Orchestration". Here they look at the impact of using multi-channel media. They also drew some clear conclusions which they saw as applying broadly:

• Multi-channel campaigns are more effective than single-channel ones.

• TV is still the most effective medium at driving both hard and soft measures, but press and outdoor can play an extremely important role as a lead advertising medium on a plan.

• Three is the most effective number of advertising media to drive hard business measures, but the more the merrier for intermediate measures.

• Advertising coupled with a sales conversion channel, such as direct marketing or sales promotion, is the most effective combination to drive hard business success.

• Advertising coupled with sponsorship or PR are the two most effective combinations to drive intermediate metrics, such as brand affinity.

The IPA challenged the idea that integration is always best; campaigns that are not integrated, but for which each channel is planned and executed separately, can be extremely effective, and since they may take much less marketing resource to manage, should be considered a useful route to pursue.

Both reports reinforce the importance of TV as a lead medium.

But what if that is not available to you? Then the IPA suggests that press and outdoor can be an able substitute.

There are many more that could be used including other types of traditional media, as well as digital. You should remember the importance of face to face contact as a persuader.

The IPA suggests that you should look to three channels working together.

You can mix and match from a vast range of opportunities. The aim, overall, is to run media at the same time, to bring to bear the impact of repetition.

On top, of course, of any external media you might use, there is a wide variety of "Point of Purchase" available at various levels within the store.

ACTION: Explore stacking media within your core area.

Messaging

Back to Ehrenburg who you first met in the Introduction.

Having analysed a number of campaigns, Ehrenburg concludes that the role here of advertising is to deliver salience. That is to say, to bring the brand into focus much more in an area.

In essence, he would say, it does not actually matter too much what you say, but how often you say it.

The discussion paper given to Ehrenburg Institute supporters (the likes of P&G and Kelloggs) concluded that an agency brief should focus more on cut-through than on a persuasive selling proposition.

Summary

So where are we in the area of media outside of a store?

- *There is the magic number 3;*

- *Then you need to remember a focus on cut through;*

- *When looking to promotion techniques as part of this it is important to remember that a message was much more likely to be opened or read if there was a coupon attached.*

POP and other "in-store media"

The shopper has a long and varied path to reach the exact point at which they stand in front of a real, or virtual, display of your product, and take the decision to buy. Inside and associated with the store, there are many media available, more or less official from the point of view of store central.

It is too easy to see your product as something like a magnet drawing people in. It is a better metaphor if you see a shopper a little like a random particle with many options as to where to go and what to buy. Some of these location options may not stock the product, some may not sell it. Very few products are destinations.

Often it is easier to see yourself as reducing the chances of your product NOT selling, than actually promoting the sale. This leads you to focus on distribution, availability and display. But then before that, you need to build the brand so people actually recognise your pack and what it is, not just let their eye skate over it to a pack, product or service they do recognise. This book explains what has to be done to secure that first recognition by the shopper-or buyer if B2B (Business to Business), whatever you are selling. For B2C (Business to Consumer) the shopper's family and friends will need to have that same awareness and for B2B those around the buyer will also need that recognition to ensure a sale.

The Influence of the Web

IGD Shoppervista (2013) figures revealed that almost a third of shoppers – up from 6% in 2010 – used the internet to go shopping to find the stores offering the best food and grocery deals. This rises to 41% in the 18-24 year old category, and almost half (48%) in families with children under 5.

The research also found that:

- They were using technology to inspire them with 47% looking for recipes online, and 23% watching food channels.

- 32% would like to be alerted to deals on their mobile phone when passing a food or grocery store.

- 19% are already using a price comparison site.

- Using technology saves them time (74%), money (69%) and helps them follow a healthier diet (49%).

The internet also represents an opportunity to advertise to shoppers. On the face of it, this would be online POP. There are, though, pitfalls in deciding where you place the messaging. Browsing on the web is not the same as in a store.

The retailers are keen to get investment in their online site, and if you choose to follow this route, you may find this research from Evolution Insights of interest. They track the way that people look at a screen when they are buying online. This research is based on retailer web sites.

Front Page and Login

Common assumptions: This is the best place for your top offers, shoppers expect to see them at this stage. FMCG's must support for their strongest promotions of the year.

Research suggests: Page footfall does not necessarily equate to interaction with marketing initiatives – shoppers are very focussed on logging in, booking their delivery slot and starting their shop.

Favourites

Common assumptions: This section is used by most shoppers to purchase regular items. It is a good place to position initiatives and alternatives to influence decision making.

Research suggests: The most likely to engage with favourites are frequent weekly online shoppers who use it primarily as a shortcut to buy the regular staples. They often move away from the favourites after this, and complain about the length and lack of personalisation. 1 in 3 don't use favourites at all.

Key Word Search

Common assumptions: Very powerful position for shopper marketing as shoppers typically search for specific items they already intend to purchase. Those who recalled marketing and offers complained about low relevance.

Research suggests: Shoppers often search for specific brands by keyword, or use keyword search as a quicker way just to find the right department. Evolution suggest there is a significant opportunity to improve here.

The Checkout

Common assumptions: Best area for impulse purchases and new products. Relevance is key. Evolution find impulse purchasing is very low.

Research suggests: Better used as a reminder - "have you forgotten...?" Shoppers are focused on reviewing their basket and entering financial details.

Point of purchase store media

POP is defined as "advertising at or near the point of purchase or on the path to purchase designed to draw attention to, highlight significant benefits of, or communicate an offer on a particular product or service, to communicate with and affect the behaviour of the shopper".

Share of the advertising market now attributable to POP is estimated to be close to 8.5%.

Brands are now spending the same levels on insights as they are on design – 10% of overall budgets, with 60% going on manufacturing and 20% on implementation.

Many major brands are planning only modest increases in POP spending between now and 2015 – a result of amending in-store strategies rather than budgetary pressures due to economic conditions. 35% said they expected to spend more on POP than in 2011. Over a third of retailers surveyed in the industry study said they anticipate spending more on POP in 2013 than the last two years.

Less than 25% of brands and retailers surveyed currently assess the success of their POP display programmes, either in terms of sales uplift or brand awareness. Of those that do, 86% said that they use sales uplift as their main criteria.

POPAI figures are skewed to the printed and broadcast word. There are other ways of getting the message across, and if you consider what consumers say about their influences, you should definitely include sampling and experiential as being extremely important in delivering change.

The last 30 yards

A vital role for marketing spend is the "last 30 yards". This is often referred to as the distance from the stock room to the shelf. It is not a coincidence that this is also the distance that the shopper walks to be in front of the facing. Somehow, though, this marketing imperative seems to get lost in the split between the sales and marketing initiatives.

What goes wrong, and why? In the case of the web, this applies per click. How can you improve the perceived presence of your own product best? In the Path to Purchase this last 30 yards is vital in getting the maximum from your listing. In this role the shopper and the store are equally important.

1. POP is a message to the store, as much as it is to the shopper, that here they have something important that needs to be taken care of. Provided, of course, that you tell the store why it is important to them. Check the Pepperami research later in this chapter.

2. POP helps to hold any additional shelf space you might have negotiated in a store – in tests with one of the world leading canned product companies, a bay marking shelf strip supporting a promotion delivered 15% more sales than a store where this was not in place. This is a direct result of space not being over-flowed into by adjacencies as well as the additional prominence of the product.

3. POP is a message to the shopper – exactly what, and where we are just going to look at.

POP can offer, therefore twice as much benefit for the store as for the shopper, but only if the store knows how important your product can be to their shoppers.

As a general rule, miss no opportunity to communicate to the store as well as the shopper. Innocent were very pleased with the performance of their on-outer offer to shelf fillers, where they could collect for free goods with proofs of purchase from the outer. They thought that this meant their outers shifted first, and received the maximum space. The fast turnover of store staff in this area guarantees regular new customers for this particular offer.

A few facts to throw into meetings (POPAI Grocery Display Effectiveness Survey);

- In a typical main shop store such as Tesco and Asda people take an average of 1.45 seconds to make a purchase. In the Co-op it is only 1.24.

- The total main shop time on average for a main shop is 46 minutes, and for the Co-op 24 minutes.

- The POP messages that converted most to sales after shoppers had engaged with POP were these. Consider adding POP if you have any of these to talk about:
  - Price reduction/new lower price 69%
  - Extra free product 60%
  - Price reduction + quantity discount 55%
  - Loyalty points: quantity discount 52%
  - Quantity discount with multibuy 46%
  - Quantity discount 40%
  - Quantity discount + value/saving msg 33%
  - New + price reduction 33%

- Displays that are large and vertically positioned can also be used to trigger an echo or subliminal "fear flight" response.

Over millions of years humans have become good at recognising movement or shapes that move horizontally across their field of vision. Even though most POP displays do not incorporate movement, a vertically blocked display can achieve better results because it stimulates these "autonomic" responses.

Evolution has given humans a fantastically powerful memory for images and most of our shopping is done entirely using images. Once the shopper has "engaged" with the POP display there is less than 1 second in which to deliver the key message and the products' USP to the shopper.

Primary text should always to be kept to an absolute minimum. After all, shoppers are walking down the aisle at 0.5 to 1.5 mph. If the key message is to promote a new product then the single word "NEW" is all that's needed to achieve the shopper engagement. Short words are easier and quicker to assimilate. For example, the research shows that "£1"achieves better results than "double loyalty points for two packs."

What can you use?

Point of Purchase can be very cheap – but also very expensive, if it does not get placed. Storecheck, and POPAI have measured many elements of POP. A review that I did with POPAI over 10 years of case studies, did not find one study that did not deliver a significant uplift.

The POPAI "Grocery Effectiveness Survey" reinforces the so-called three golden rules of display – Position, Position, Position. Marketers have acknowledged the importance of obtaining the right location for POP displays in-store for some time. For the first time, the study has provided some clearer direction about the correlation between the location of POP displays within grocery retailing in physical proximity to the shopper and the resulting impact it has on them, in terms of impact, engagement and conversion. POP displays located above the head of shoppers scored particularly poorly; shoppers rarely look up. The impact ratio for above head height POP was just 4% whilst the conversion ratio was only marginally better (12%).

The closer to the product, the better

Tesco stopped the rollout of their store screens simply because they did not work. Bags of impact, but in such a densely media rich environment, one message was swiftly replaced by another. In any case, who has time to block the aisle for 15 seconds while you look at a message?

What gets placed?

Following through on the theme of real and virtual availability, you will not be able to get anything that requires more product to fill, unless more product is physically in the store. So supplying the two together in the form of a pre-packed or a prefilled display will always get you much better compliance, even though the cost is significantly higher.

POP Placement ratios

Data	2005	2002	Grand Total
Permanent Units	61.37%	66.05%	63.71%
Flat Packed	40.73%	57.19%	48.96%
Shelf Trays	67.82%	67.20%	59.28%
Headers	67.47%	73.89%	67.33%
Prepacked Shippers	70.64%	85.61%	72.26%
Shelf Edge POP	72.97%	81.39%	79.29%
Hanging Signs	74.50%	68.87%	66.97%
Total	**65.07%**	**68.87%**	**66.97%**

Stores are short staffed, and tend to add POP towards the end of the list of priorities, which is why placement can be disappointingly low. From what you have read so far you can easily see that the 100% compliance should be in your core stores. They should be more motivated if your store contact policy has worked, and of course, will also give you the best ROI from placement, as well as any efforts you make to get material placed.

On the other hand...

POPAI research carried out by Storecheck and Shopper Insights with store managers, sales managers and buyers showed that buyers undervalue dramatically the impact of POP. They believed that it only added 10% to category sales. They reported that POP communication proposals were the ones most likely to fail with only 27% of them being accepted.

For sales managers POP was much more important; they felt that it contributed 32% to sales. This statistic could only be based on a feeling though, as 60% said they did not measure in any way.

Store managers felt that POP contributed 46% to normal category sales, and 56% to promotion sales. This is a huge contrast with the buyers, and even with sales managers. Store managers, of course, are in the best possible position to know what is actually going on.

The manager reports are also much more in line with the dunnhumby view that "calls to action at the facing are often more powerful than discounts" (IPA report "Discounting in the Downturn, Shrewd or Crude").

Dunnhumby are clearly fans of POP material, in particular in the small store environment, and looking at these figures from RMI, it is easy to see why.

Media for various product	Immediate Uplift	Residual
Radio	18.80%	12.20%
Radio and shelf talkers	35.40%	11.40%
Radio and screens	24.00%	14.40%
Radio, screens and shelf talkers	19.00%	10.30%
Small talker	7.00%	8.50%
Shelf talkers	21.50%	5.80%
Shelf talkers and tear off talkers	23.60%	7.40%
Screens and shelf talkers	19.60%	6.50%
Screens, wobblers and bus stop	21.60%	5.80%
Right angled talker and mailshot	7.20%	17.30%

Stacking Messaging

RMI handle all of the media booking for Co-op stores. These small stores have a broad range of applicable media managed at least in part centrally. RMI also manage availability of the Co-op store by store sales data. They are therefore, as indeed are dunnhumby for Tesco, in a unique position to see the results of applied marketing spend.

It seems clear that in-store media can have a long-lasting influence on the brand. It is also clear that there is significant variance between the various implementations depending on the brand and, of course, any competitive activity.

As such, like any direct media, you should seek to trial options using epos data as your success measure. Other media available include store loyalty card work, as an alternative to discounts or joint purchases of various types.

Getting POP placed

The single important piece of information for all parties is a knowledge of how much POP means to sales:

1. It helps you to put the right degree of emphasis.

2. It will persuade your buyer how serious you are, and of the importance of POP in a more profitable future.

3. It will make the difference in store managers willingness to spend time.

It is staggering to think that so much POP is produced by so many buyers, who hardly value it at all. But at the store end a manager could have 20-30,000 POP movements every month. Not a surprise then that only POP they feel to be important actually ends up in front of the shopper, rather than the dumpster.

Storecheck ran a research project with Unilever in the Co-op for Pepperami, reported by POPAI. This added an additional front reservoir in the chiller, making better use of the shelf allocated, and increasing standout. This was accompanied into store and placed by a team, so usage was monitored. After a period, the control stores also gained the unit.

The result, a 20% increase in sales in both as a result of the use of the display. At the time the control stores came on board the trial stores were told the results. Control stores received just the units.

Storecheck tracked results seven months later to find that 88% of the trial stores that knew the impact of the unit had kept it in place! That's 50% more than the control stores managed, even though their units were two months older.

There were a number of morals here:

- 100% of store managers said they would be more or much more likely to place the POP had they been made aware of the effect on sales. Demonstrably they kept it in place much longer when they did know.

- 20% of stores did not have the glass fronts to the chiller that the design of the tray required – but still received a unit they could not use. Even a research project can be thrown by The Rumsfeld Effect.

- POP – as with anything is a message to the store. If you throw it at them without telling them what they are getting, it would be perverse to expect them to value it any more than you did. The POP needs to convey what it will do for them too.

Chapter 9

Becoming a Local Brand Leader

Core stores service areas with a higher proportion of the right kind of people. They are exactly the people you would want to reach with your advertising and promotion messaging. For many companies, 15% of core stores can represent 40% of total sales, and of course, promotionally, this percentage is even higher. Look at the POP and other media chapter to see how you can cost effectively target growth around these stores.

The areas local to these stores can also return more from investment. You should find that you will have a couple of Tesco stores, a Sainsbury and an Asda listed in the area. There are, though, smaller stores you will not be in. As you grow the area, many more stores will become profitable, and the increased awareness that the increased ranging will also give will augment the impression of your importance.

Increased store listings can be achieved in all major stores, either centrally, or by local negotiation. It's a question of understanding the process for each group.

I'm not going to go into all the details on impacting on a shopper and looking at the many ways that they could be reached and influenced.

I am going to give you a few very simple guidelines that will allow you to take the right decision about where to invest.

1. Shopping is over in micro-seconds

Most decisions are based on decision trees that people bring into a store, either on paper, or in their heads. You have to break these if you want them to try something new.

2. If they can't see it, it won't make an impact

Shoppers actually look a little bit downwards as they track down the aisle. We are all very well trained not to make eye contact. They don't look at the floor, and they don't look at headers so if you want to stop their progress it has to be at eye level.

3. Tasteful doesn't hack it

A pack flash carefully designed to blend in to the pack misses the point. You are trying to get to new people. Only existing customers will actually look closely enough to get the message.

4. A half empty shelf looks, and behaves, like a fully empty shelf

This is particularly the case if it's a lower shelf, and you are as tall as I am (over 6 foot). So the fact that there is one single soldier guarding the space does NOT mean the shopper will stop and buy it. You have to aim for better.

5. People navigate using stimuli from brands they know well, even though they may not actually buy the brand

Be in the right place, or off the page. Shelf signage such as bus stops for key brands will prompt shopping, and not just for the brand featured.

6. KISS (Keep It Simple Stupid)

Adding really simple words like "NEW" when you are, and "FREE" when you add something extra makes a difference.

7. Stacking

Aim to deliver a very high share of voice (SOV) whenever you bring activity into an area. This is a measure of how much media share you have compared to your market share (SOM). A Nielsen study confirmed that:

- SOV to SOM ratio is key, if not the best indicator of what level of media support is needed to drive share growth.

- 96% of leading brands that grew share maintained SOV/SOM ratios exceeding 100%.

- There is a substantial lag effect resulting from SOV/SOM ratio changes and actual market share impacts.

- SOV/SOM must be sustained for a long period to drive share changes.

- The greater uniformity/equality that exists among the competition on the quality of advertising and brand benefits, the stronger the correlation of SOV/SOM.

- Brands with news or high growth categories get a better return on increased SOV/SOM ratio.

The following circumstances require greater SOV/SOM ratio to grow:

- New brands generally need a disproportionate ratio (150 to 200 indexes) to get a foothold and grow;

- Longer purchase cycles;

- New brands without a quality or equity difference.

The theory of SOV/SOM ratio does not hold for the following situations:

- A major price change by one brand;

- A brand pre-launch or significant new innovation;

- Entry of a significant, dynamic brand;

- Much more compelling message, copy or creative for one brand;

- Dramatically poorer brand image or equity.

Chapter 10
Things to Do Today

If you have read the book so far, I hope that you will have been convinced that the best way to plan to grow your brand to shoppers is to make the best use of data that is around you and just needs to be brought together. This means seeing the brand as your shoppers see it, the way your brand is actually available to them via your retailers, and the demand by region and by store. With these core elements you can determine where, and how, you can advertise, and promote with the expectation of gaining the best possible impact for your brand budget.

In the past, you might have been excused for thinking that this kind of information is much too expensive, or time consuming to ever be able to afford.

I have been to some pains to seek out what can be done using the latest techniques, in order to deliver insights previously unaffordable except to the very largest brands.

Pull your data together to measure the past – and the future

Moving on to the core areas; those with more of the right people to hear and respond to your message. The easiest way to determine this is by integrating your epos data with geo-demographic data, regionality and store size. In the UK this is developed from census data by a range of companies. It needs to be attributed properly to stores, since where people shop is about access, and not distance. As an example, if a motorway runs right past the door, a store is effectively closer in time than a city centre store that might be closer in distance. It is time, and not distance, that determines convenience. This approach is only useful for destination stores - the top 3,000 in the UK. Outside of this, store footfall tends to be determined by passing traffic, whether by car or on foot.

Companies like the British Population Survey and retailvitalstatistics.com can deliver pre-packaged insights in this area.

Your core area will over-perform against promotions, discounts and advertising investment provided of course that you maximise your real availability (more stores, more stock in those stores, more signage and greater space and prominence).

Maximising Discount Sales

There is a simple message here. Discounts really work, but they need to be seen as part of a strategy. If you don't make money while you are discounting, you need to innovate until you do. Backing out is unlikely to be a viable option,

The biggest issue in managing promotions is managing promotion availability. Critical to this is Day 1 availability in store, making core store managers, and supply chain personnel aware that it is critical for their success that they improve availability for your products over the competitors. This is all about knowing where the core stores are, and how much stock they need to have.

There is nothing wrong at all with stacking promotions on top of discounts provided, of course, you make money and you get your store supply right. Examples include sampling or on-pack alongside discounting, and couponing in the locality and the store when you are not.

Manage your core stores very tightly – they offer provable growth, and techniques that work here can be used elsewhere.

Generating growth and building brands

Companies carry out relatively little research. Many marketers are unaware of the zynergy available in the core areas they will typically work in without any cross benefits building up. The result? Store stockouts and irritated managers and shoppers.

Bring some marketing spend into a joint pot. Promote to shoppers when you are on discount; they will be grateful, they will tell their friends and their Facebook buddies. Manage your stock then, and between discounts you have a broad range of activities that are less expensive, and relatively more successful than discounting.

Behave like a brand leader

....but only where you have a realistic chance of becoming one.

Build your Core – manage every input into it and make partners out of colleagues and all your customers. They will give you free publicity, free display space, free promotions, and extra sales and margin. Bear in mind that you would want to have six messages on the way to a sale – three media supplemented by store and near store messaging.

Develop a communication strategy to all the stakeholders, stores centrally and locally, shoppers and consumers. Give them all feedback appropriate to their needs. Hyper-local advertising is the growth area for the future. Use it. Remember that your Share of Voice in your core area should exceed your target market share.

Chapter 11
Case Studies

These case studies revolve around the use of advertising and promotion techniques applied down to individual area and store level. These are separate from the kinds of support that the store offers themselves, such as those outlined earlier by RMI in the Co-op, or, indeed, those typically offered within store such as aisle based tastings. They are reproduced ©Core2Store.com who manage and measure, coordinated core area and store support.

The concept of stacking is very important

Coupon campaigns work in combination with core stores contact (email, telephone and mail). Store managers like coupons, and they like to know when they will impact on their store. The coupon activity here, a doordrop around core stores, lead to a period of sustained growth in these stores.

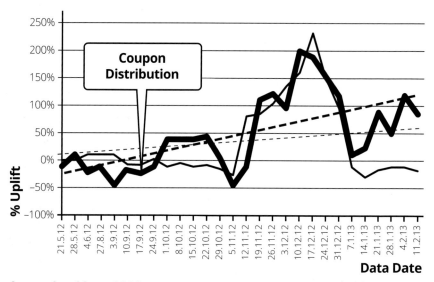

Source:Core2Store 2013

The major growth here happens AFTER the couponing and after the promotion, and is a result of the zynergy of the advertising message, and, in particular, the store use of additional space and better managed stock.

(The chart shows the progress of the stores in terms of average sales across the course of the activity and afterwards. The darker line represents control stores, the lighter, trial).

On-pack messaging works: You have already been advised of the reported impact of the simple word "NEW". This message won't work for more than 3 months. So what else can you do? Well, given that redemptions are low, you have a wide leeway. In particular on pack offers, which can be either affixed to the pack centrally, or in a core store with the permission of the manager, typically with the help of a field team.

Here is one of a number of such charts, showing the impact of on-pack messaging. In this case these have been added to core stores, and the chart shows the uplift from the previous period. This is a new product launch, for a cat feed product, ultima. A new entrant in a very crowded market place. This slice is taken about 3 months from the start.

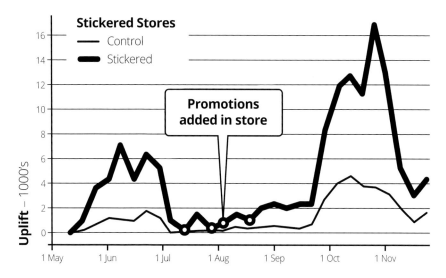

Source:Core2Store 2013

Compared to control stores you can see the rapid growth inspired by using just a simple "Get £1 back plus a free gift". The very low redemptions make the major cost for this the sticker.

The technique brings in more people, as can be proved by feedback from **www.yousay.org**, the site redeeming the claims. Yousay is a service specifically designed to turn shopper offers into information via branded microsites. Yousay feedback revealed that over 90% of the people coming in were new to the brand.

This approach clearly appeals to different shoppers than the discount a few weeks before. These people stay to carry on buying, and growth after the next promotion has continued undisturbed.

In-store POS can range from simple such as shelf edge, to complicated, such as shippers. In the chart you can see the impact of simple shelf edge material supporting a promotion. Here the scale is average sales. The product was a leading brand canned food.

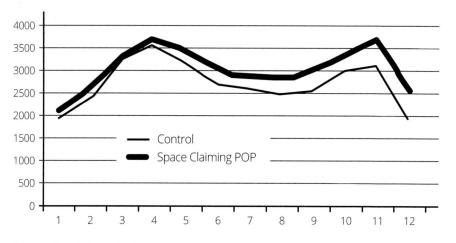

The Impact of Space Claiming POP

Source:Core2Store 2013

All of this activity was related, at some point or another, to a price promotion. In all cases, the use of additional techniques also built promotion sales as well as leading to growth AFTER the discount left the shelf.

It is also important to note that every one of these was accompanied by a store communication package. Two carried out by telephone and store callage, one by telephone and mail.

Chapter 12
Useful Resources

BCS www.bcindex.co.uk

The British Consumer Index is based on British Population Survey data and provides "reference" up to date information on the population of Great Britain. It can be used for insight, segmentation, modelling and as a means of better understanding and interpreting on-line survey results. Data is gathered by actually going out and talking to people in their own homes, between 6,000 and 8,000 of them every month.

Core2Store core2store.com

Identify, deliver, and measure stacked media and messaging into core stores and areas. Set up and manage a communications strategy to the store and the area, designed to build consumer demand and store supply concurrently. Develop key availability by also managing and sorting store issues such as restarting non-selling stores, and gaining more distribution.

IPM www.theipm.org.uk

The Institute of Promotional Marketing is the UK trade association which represents brand owners, agencies and service providers which use or create promotional marketing.

POPAI   www.popai.co.uk

The not-for-profit trade association dedicated to the point-of-purchase (POP) industry and shopper marketing. POPAI UK & Ireland conducts research, organises conferences, industry awards, seminars and best practice programmes to benefit its members who include retailers, brands, agencies, and manufacturers. Research includes the Grocery Display Effectiveness survey.

Retail Vital Statistics   retailvitalstatistics.com

Integrated information provider, in the cloud, to your desktop or your mobile. RVS information identifies issues and opportunities at store and area level for brands and retailers needing to target shopper and consumer opportunity delivered down to store level.

RMI http://rmi.co/

Work closely with retailers to assist them in understanding all of the many channels that they have available, to not only create an additional income stream but generate a robust incremental sales uplift. This is then made available through software, allowing brands and the retailer to see and understand all the media channels available, making it much easier for brands to buy into the media channels.

SBXL   www.sbxl.com

Shopper Behaviour Xplained – work primarily, but not solely, from video footage taken from the facing. They see their role as interpreting the opportunity in an area of the store, and for a particular brand, by comparison with what can be achieved based on well observed and documented behaviour.

SpectrumInsight   www.spectrum-insight.com

Build insight for action from listening to feedback from shoppers and consumers on-line wherever they offer their opinion. The insight, unlike normal market research, is based on unprompted opinion data-mined from millions of lines of shared opinions. It is therefore both quality, and quantity in one, which is why it is called Qualimetrics.

VCG Promorisk   www.vcgpromorisk.com

VCG helps multinational brands manage the risks associated with promotional campaigns of all types - from money-off coupons, instant win schemes and free gift mail-ins, to online and mobile promotions for one all-inclusive Fixed Fee. With the VCG Fixed Fee, you know in advance exactly what the promotion will cost – so you don't have to compromise.

ISBN: 978-1494241896